LANGUAGE ARTS

WILLIAM & MARY

THE CENTER FOR GIFTED EDUCATION

Patterns of Change

Second Edition

Student Guide

Grades 4-6

Cover image © JupiterImages Corporation.

Kendall Hunt
publishing company

www.kendallhunt.com
Send all inquiries to:
4050 Westmark Drive
Dubuque, IA 52004-1840
1-800-542-6657

Center for Gifted Education
College of William & Mary
PO Box 8795
Williamsburg, VA 23187-8795
757-221-2362
www.cfge.wm.edu

Funded by the Jacob K. Javits Program, United States Department of Education, under a subcontract from the Washington-Saratoga-Warren-Hamilton-Essex BOCES, Saratoga Springs, New York.

ISBN 978-0-7575-6606-6

Printed by: Lightning Source
United States of America
Batch number: 426606

Printed in the United States of America

Contents

LESSON 5

LESSON 6

LESSON 7

Letter to Student

Dear Student:

You are participating in a special language arts unit called *Patterns of Change.* It is organized around the concept of cyclic patterns of change and has many activities designed to help you understand this concept.

A wide variety of literature will allow you to explore cyclic patterns of change. The literature will stimulate discussion, writing, listening, vocabulary study, and research activities. In class, we will read and discuss short pieces of literature including poems and short stories. You will also read two novels. To clarify your thinking and to help prepare for written and oral assignments, you will keep a journal. As you read the literature, you will respond to it and think critically about it by analyzing ideas, vocabulary, and structure.

The purpose of this book is to provide you with additional materials that you will need to participate in the unit. All of the unit short stories and poems are contained in this book, as well as activities related to all literature selections.

During the course of the unit, you will be using several models to help organize your thinking. They include:

1. Literature Web Model
2. Vocabulary Web Model
3. Metaphor Analysis Model
4. Hamburger Model for Persuasive Writing
5. Writing Process Model
6. Reasoning Model
7. Research Model

Your teacher will explain how these models work and how you can use them as you read the unit literature and complete the required activities.

Sincerely,

Curriculum Development Team
Center for Gifted Education at The College of William & Mary

Glossary of Literary Terms

The following list contains a selection of literary terms which may be useful for students to understand in the discussion of literature in the unit.

Allegory: a narrative that is an extended metaphor. Allegories are written in the form of fables, parables, poems, stories, and almost any other style or genre. In an allegory, the characters, setting, and other parts of the story have both literal and symbolic meanings.

Alliteration: the repetition of consonant sounds at the beginning of words or stressed syllables. A poet may use alliteration to dramatize action or mimic actual sounds.

Antagonist: the adversary of the protagonist of a literary work.

Character: a person portrayed in an artistic piece, such as a drama or novel.

Climax: the decisive moment of a narrative or drama, usually the most intense part of the story and occurring near the end.

Denouement: the resolution of a narrative or drama, following the climax.

Dialogue: the conversation between characters in a narrative or drama.

Figurative language: language that is not literal. Figurative language does not mean exactly what it says, but instead forces the reader to make an imaginative leap in order to comprehend an author's point.

Flashback: a literary device that allows the author to present events that happened before the time of the current events in the story. Flashback techniques include memories, dreams, and stories of the past told by characters.

Foreshadowing: the organization and presentation of events in a story in such a way that the reader is given clues about what will happen later in the work.

Free verse: verse with no meter, variable line length, and either no rhyme or an unpatterned use of rhyme.

Imagery: the use of language to create vivid sensory impressions in the imagination.

Metaphor: a type of figurative language which compares two things by saying one *is* the other. (Example: The girl is a ray of sunshine.)

Motivation: the desire or reasons that drive a character to act.

Narrative: a story or account telling about events that may be fictional or true.

Narrator/narrative voice: one who tells a story; the speaker or the "voice" of an oral or written work.

Personification: figurative language in which human characteristics are given to animals, ideas, or objects.

Plot: the series of events that make up a story.

Point of view: the frame of reference from which the events of a story are conveyed to the reader; the "vantage point" from which the narrative is written.

Protagonist: the main character or lead figure in a novel, play, story, or poem.

Rising action: a related series of events in a story that build toward the point of greatest interest.

Setting: the time, place, and circumstances in which a narrative, drama, or movie takes place.

Simile: a type of figurative language which compares two things by using the words *like* or *as*. (Example: Her skin was as white as snow.)

Stanza: a group of lines of verse (usually not less than four), arranged according to a definite scheme; normally forms a division of a song or poem.

Structure: order of the parts of a story or poem, and the relationship of the parts to each other and to the entire work. Structural devices include such things as time order, comparison, cause/effect, spatial order, and repetition.

Symbol: an image, word, or object that stands for something greater than itself; the image is usually visible, but what it represents is often invisible. For example, the flag is a symbol of patriotism.

Theme: the central idea of a poem, short story, or novel.

Tone: the writer's attitude toward the readers and subject; the writer's mood or moral view.

Voice: the tone, attitude, or personality of the speaker as it reveals itself directly or indirectly in the narrative.

Models

The following pages include information about some models that you can use to help organize your thinking.

The Literature Web Model

The Literature Web is designed to guide you in interpreting your reading by helping you connect your personal response with elements of the text. The web may also be used as a tool for discussion. The kinds of observations that belong in each of the five parts of the web are as follows:

1. *Key words:* interesting, unfamiliar, striking, or particulary important words and phrases within the text
2. *Feelings:* your feelings and the specific text details that inspire them; the characters' feelings; and the feelings that you infer the author intended to inspire
3. *Ideas:* major themes and main ideas of the text; key concepts
4. *Images and symbols:* notable sensory images in the text; "pictures" the text creates in your mind and the details that inspire them; symbols for abstract ideas
5. *Structure:* the formal elements of the writing and their contribution to meaning; including such things as time order, comparison, cause/effect, spatial order, use of voice, use of figurative language, and repetition

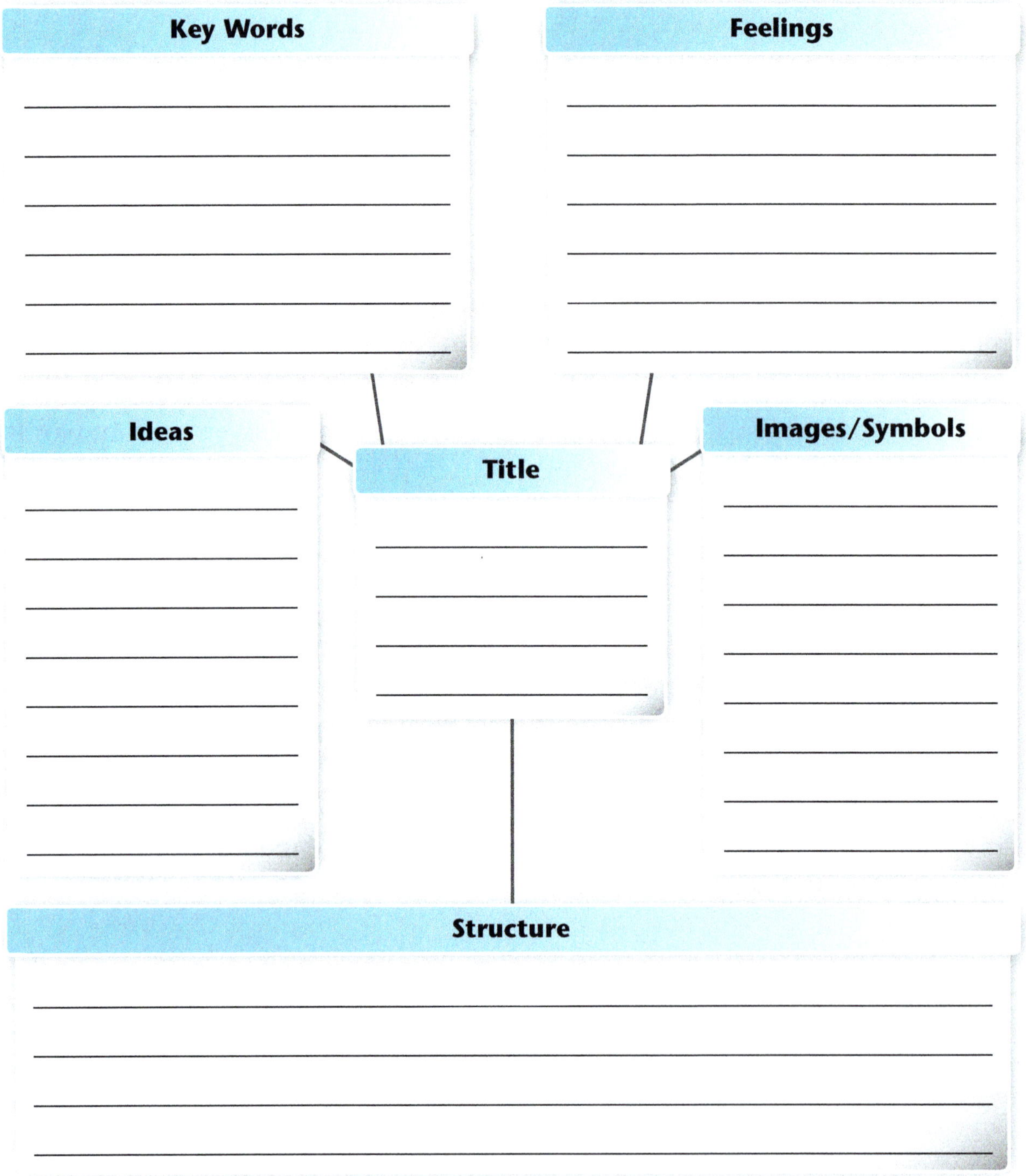

Key Words

Feelings

Ideas

Title

Images/Symbols

Structure

Figure 1-1: Literature Web Model

The Vocabulary Web Model

The Vocabulary Web is a tool for exploring a word in depth. Find the definition of the word and its part of speech, synonyms and antonyms, word stems, and origin. Then identify word families by finding at least three other words that use one or more of your word's stems. Create an example to explain your word (a sentence, an analogy, a picture or diagram, etc.). Use the Vocabulary Web to organize your responses.

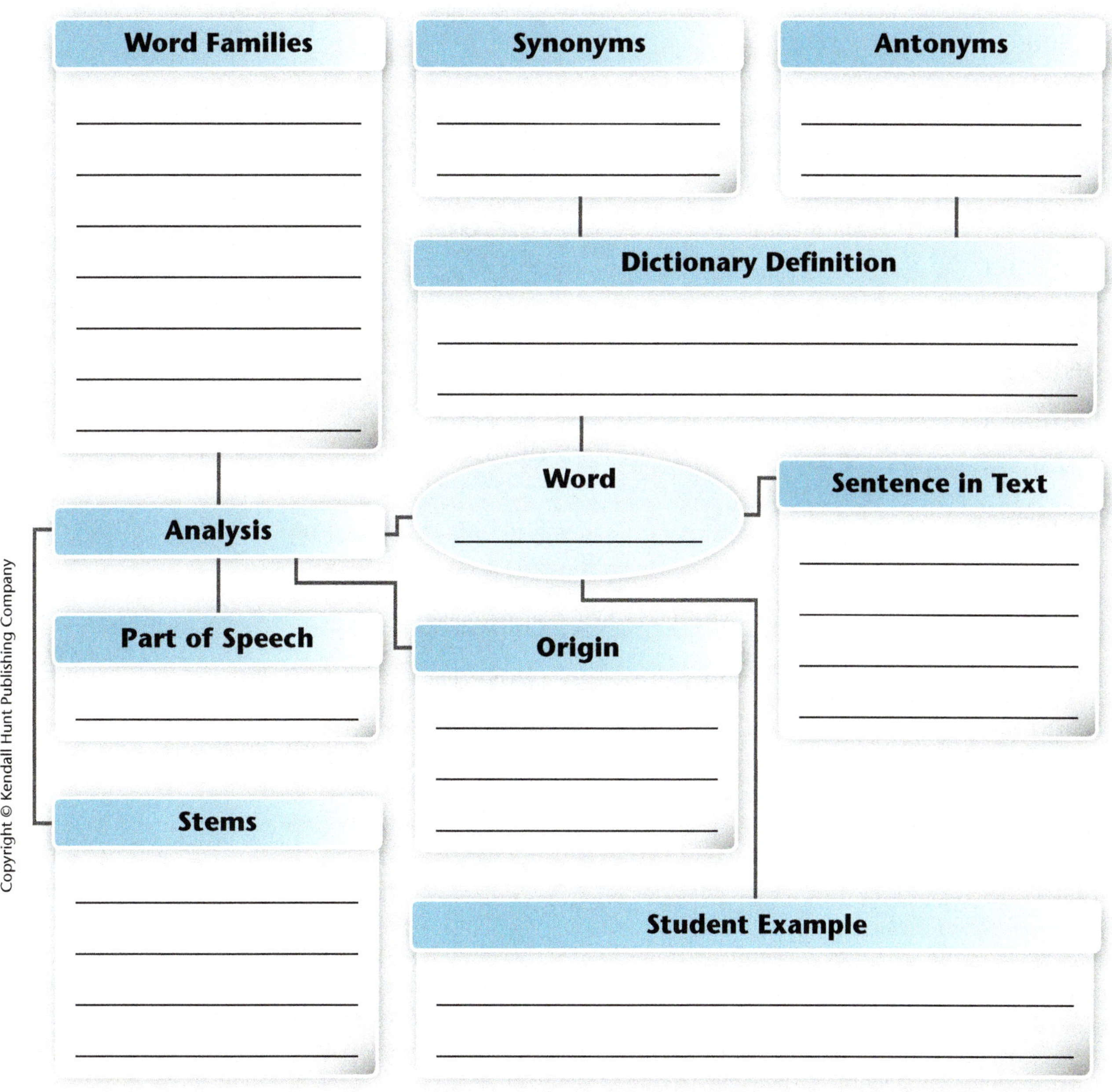

Figure 1-2: Vocabulary Web Model

Unit vocabulary words you may want to explore include:

From "On the Pulse of Morning":

brutishness

mendicant

mastodon

yoked

Literary Terms (from Lesson 4):

antagonist

character

climax

denouement

flashback

foreshadowing

metaphor

narrator/narrative voice

plot

protagonist

rising action

setting

simile

symbol

theme

tone/mood

From "A Day":

amethyst

bobolink

stile

From "The Sleeping Flowers":

inquire

quaint

reverent

From "The Wind Is Blowing West":

boisterous

diffuse

From "A Bouquet of Wild Flowers":

cultivated

proverb

republic

fundamental

From *My Daniel*:

accustomed
arrogant
banister
cache
chinook
concoctions
conveyor
cynical
embossed
exclusive
gnarled
hobbled
hoisted
hysterical
involuntarily
kerosene
kindred
mortgage
ornery
petrified
pier
pleurisy
plied
poised
prospector
purveyor
resurrected
sanctuary
sauerkraut
saurian
scudded
sheepishly
skewering
unruly
wallows

From "Walking":

aphids
audible
communal
elemental
intuition

From Sonnet II:

besiege
succession
thriftless

Metaphor Analysis Model

A metaphor is a type of figurative language which compares two things by saying one is the other. For example, you might say that your friend's smile is a rainbow, or that your bunny's tail is a cotton ball.

A metaphor has three parts:

- The *topic* is what the comparison is mainly about.
- The *vehicle* is the object to which the topic is compared.
- The *ground* is the basis for comparison, or how the topic and vehicle are alike.

This is the Metaphor Chart. The three sections show the topic, vehicle, and ground of the comparison. You can use this chart to explore the parts of any metaphor.

Figure 1-3: Metaphor Analysis Model

TOPIC of the comparison	VEHICLE (what the topic is compared to)	GROUND (characteristics the topic and vehicle share)

The Hamburger Model for Persuasive Writing

The Hamburger Model uses a sandwich as a metaphor to help you construct a paragraph or essay. Begin by stating your point of view on the issue in question (the top bun). Then provide reasons, or evidence, to support your claim; you should try to incorporate at least three supporting reasons (the "patties"). Elaboration on the reasons provides additional details (the "fixings"). A concluding sentence or paragraph wraps up the piece of writing (the bottom bun).

Figure 1-4: Hamburger Model for Persuasive Writing

Introduction
(State your opinion.)

____

____

Elaboration	**Elaboration**	**Elaboration**
______	______	______
______	______	______
______	______	______
Reason	**Reason**	**Reason**
______	______	______
______	______	______
______	______	______
Elaboration	**Elaboration**	**Elaboration**
______	______	______
______	______	______
______	______	______

Conclusion

____

____

The Reasoning Model

In the Elements of Reasoning (1992), the theorist Richard Paul provides a model of critical thinking. The model breaks down the thinking process into eight elements, or parts. Use the model and the following terms to help you think about issues and problems.

The eight Elements of Reasoning are as follows:

1. **Purpose, Goal, or End View**

   We reason for a purpose—to achieve an objective, satisfy a desire, or fulfill a need. For example, if there are no eggs or milk in your refrigerator one morning, the purpose of your reasoning would be to figure out what else to make for breakfast. If there is a problem with your purpose, then there will be problems with your reasoning. For example, if your goal is unrealistic, in conflict with your other goals, or confused in some way, then the reasoning you use to meet that goal will have problems. On the other hand, if you are clear about the purpose for your reasoning, it will help you focus your thoughts. For example, the purpose of your reasoning might be to persuade others to do something. If you are clear about this purpose, then your persuasive writing and speaking on this topic will be focused and therefore more effective. Similarly, other authors write to achieve a purpose, and when you read and listen to their work, you should be able to determine their purpose.

2. **Question at Issue (or Problem to Be Solved)**

   When we attempt to reason about something, there is at least one question at issue or problem to be solved. In fact, without question or problem, no reasoning is required! If you are not clear about what the question or problem is, it is unlikely that you will find an answer that is reasonable or suitable for your purpose. As part of the reasoning process, you should be able to state the question to be answered or the problem to be solved, such as, "What else can I use to make breakfast?" or, "Should libraries censor materials that contain objectionable language?"

Adapted from Paul, R. (1992). Critical thinking: What every person needs to survive in a rapidly changing world. *CA: Foundation for Critical Thinking.*

3. **Point of View or Frame of Reference**

As we reason about an issue, we are influenced by our own point of view. For example, parents of young children and librarians might have different points of view about censorship, or the price of a shirt may seem low to one person and high to another, depending on their frame of reference. Any problem in your point of view or frame of reference is a possible source of problems in your reasoning. Your point of view may be too narrow, not precise enough, or biased. By considering multiple points of view, you can sharpen or broaden your thinking. Similarly, in writing and speaking, you can strengthen your argument by acknowledging other points of view. In listening and reading, you need to identify the perspective of the speaker or author and understand how it affects the message.

4. **Experiences, Data, Evidence**

When we reason, we must be able to support our point of view with evidence. The use of evidence, including data from surveys or published studies, helps you to distinguish reasons from opinions, make well-reasoned judgments, and strengthen your arguments. In reading and listening, you can evaluate the strength of an argument or the validity of a statement by examining the supporting data or evidence. Experience can also provide evidence or data. For example, previous experiences making breakfast might contribute to the process of figuring out what to make for breakfast.

5. **Concepts and Ideas**

Reasoning requires the understanding and use of concepts and ideas (including definitional terms, principles, rules, or theories). When you read or listen, you can ask yourself, "What key ideas are being presented?" When you write or speak, you can examine and organize your thoughts around concepts and ideas. Some examples of concepts are freedom, friendship, and responsibility.

6. **Assumptions**

Although we may need to take some things for granted when we reason, we need to be aware of the assumptions we have made and the assumptions of others. As a writer or speaker, you make assumptions about your audience and message, and faulty assumptions can lead to problems in your reasoning. For example, you might assume that others will share your point of view, or you might refer to "First Amendment rights" without any explanation because you incorrectly assume that your audience is familiar with the First Amendment. As a reader or listener, you should be able to identify the assumptions of the writer or speaker.

7. **Inferences**

Reasoning proceeds by small mental steps called inferences. An inference is a conclusion that something is true because something else is true, or seems to be true. The inferences you make depend on the data you have and your assumptions. For example, if you see dark clouds, you might infer that it is going to rain. Or if it is now 6:45 and it takes 30 minutes to get to the movie theater, you will probably conclude that you cannot get to the theater in time for a 7:00 movie. Many inferences are justified and reasonable, but many are not. You need to distinguish between the raw data of your experiences and your inferences about those experiences. Also, be aware that the inferences you make are heavily influenced by your point of view and assumptions.

8. **Implications and Consequences**

When your reasoning takes you in a certain direction, you need to look at the implications of following that line of reasoning. When you support a certain point of view, for example, solid reasoning requires that you consider what the consequences might be of taking the course that you support. Similarly, when you read or listen to an argument, you need to ask yourself what follows from that way of thinking. You can also consider consequences of actions that characters in stories take, just as you can consider consequences of your own actions. For example, if you don't do your homework, then you might have to stay after school to complete it; or, if you water your lawn, it may not wither in the summer heat.

Figure 1-5: Wheel of Reasoning

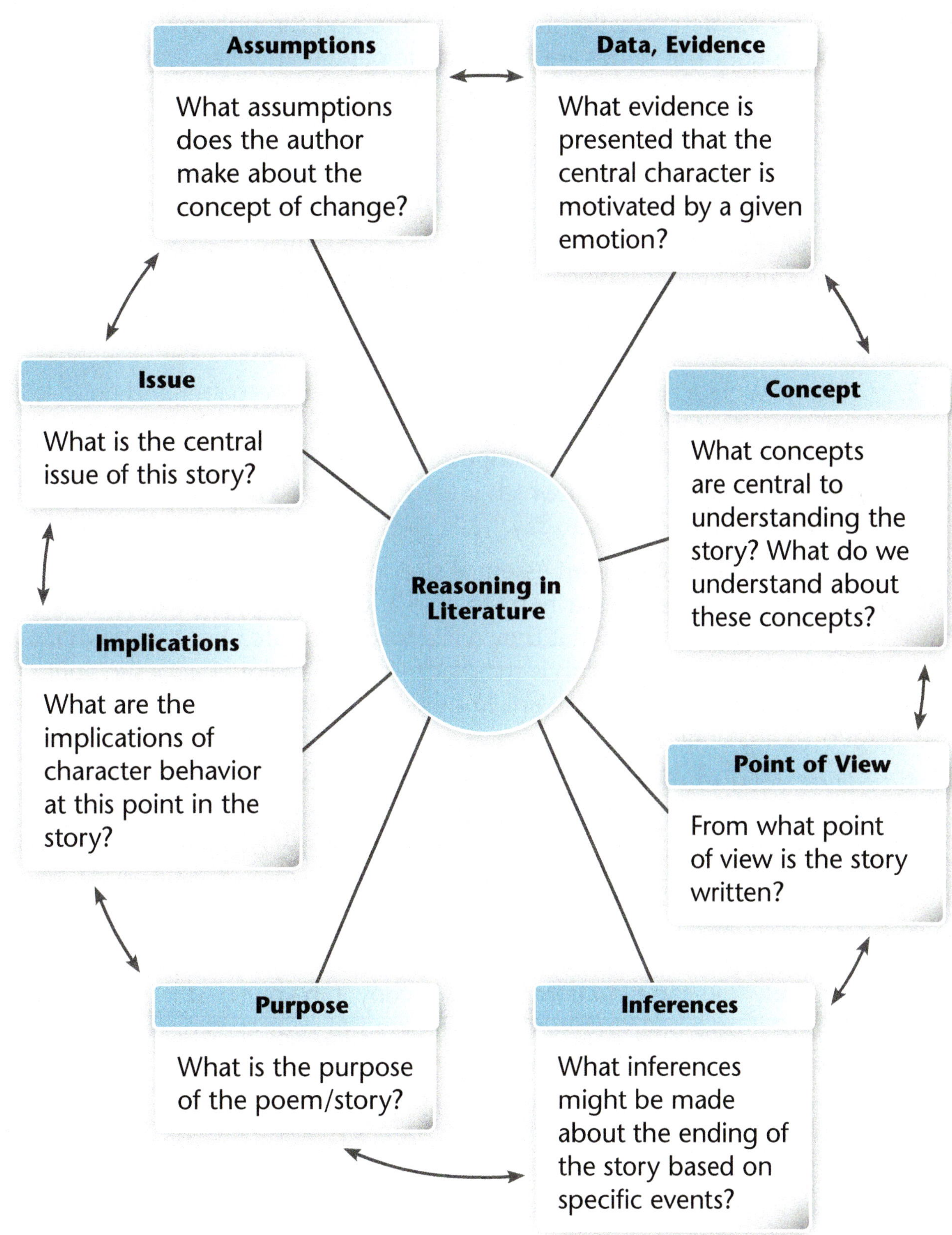

The Writing Process Model

The Writing Process describes the stages that writers go through to develop a written composition. The stages are not separate parts that writers go through from one to five; rather, writers move back and forth among the stages and use them to construct, clarify, and polish their writing. The Writing Process Model is used throughout the unit to encourage you to engage in improving your writing.

The following are the stages of the Writing Process:

1. *Prewriting:* List your ideas and begin to organize them. You may want to use a graphic organizer such as a web or Venn diagram. Graphic organizers help you to "see" what you will write about. As you write, you can add to your graphic organizer or change it.
2. *Drafting:* Write a rough draft, getting your ideas onto paper and not worrying about mechanics such as spelling, grammar, or punctuation. Some writers call this stage "composing." Sometimes this stage is a "messing around" stage in which your drafting or composing helps you to "hear" what you want to say.
3. *Revising:* Conferencing is an essential step in the revising stage. Ask people (friends, family, teachers) to read and listen to your work and to tell you what they like, what they'd like to know more about, and what they don't understand. This is the place to make major changes in your draft. Sometimes you may want to go back to the prewriting stage and redo your graphic organizer to give your paper a new structure.
4. *Editing:* After you have revised your paper, look for the small changes that will make a big difference. Check your choice of words and identify mechanical errors. After you make the changes and corrections, proofread your work one final time. You may want to ask a friend or an adult for help.
5. *Sharing or publishing:* There are numerous ways to share and to publish your work. You can bind it into a book, copy it in your best handwriting and post it on a bulletin board, read it aloud to your class or family, or make it into a gift for someone special.

The Research Model

The Research Model gives you a way to approach an issue of significance and explore it. The organization of this model is based on the major elements of the Reasoning Model.

1. **Identify your issue or problem.**
   - What is the issue or problem?
   - Who are the stakeholders and what are their positions?
   - What is *my* position on this issue?
2. **Read about your issue and identify points of view or arguments through information sources.**
   - What are my print sources?
   - What are my media sources?
   - What are my people sources?
   - What primary and secondary source documents might I use?
   - What are my preliminary findings based on a review of existing sources?
3. **Form a set of questions that can be answered by a specific set of data:**
   - What would be the results of ______________________________?
   - Who would benefit and by how much?
   - Who would be harmed and by how much?
   - My research questions: ______________________________
4. **Gather evidence through research techniques such as surveys, interviews, or analysis of primary and secondary source documents.**
   - What survey questions should I ask?
   - What interview questions should I ask?
   - What generalizations do secondary sources give?
   - What data and evidence can I find in primary sources to support different sides of the issue?

5. **Manipulate and transform data so that they can be interpreted.**
    - How can I summarize what I learned?
    - Should I develop charts, diagrams, or graphs to represent my data?
6. **Draw conclusions and make inferences.**
    - What do the data mean? How can I interpret what I found out?
    - How do the data support my original point of view?
    - How do they support other points of view?
    - What conclusions can I make about the issue?
    - What is my point of view now, based on the data?
7. **Determine implications and consequences.**
    - What are the consequences of following the point of view that I support?
    - Do I know enough or are there now new questions to be answered?
8. **Communicate your findings. (Prepare an oral presentation for classmates based on notes and written report.)**
    - What are my purpose, issue, and point of view, and how will I explain them?
    - What data will I use to support my point of view?
    - How will I conclude my presentation?

New feet within my garden go …

Emily Dickinson

New feet within my garden go,
New fingers stir the sod;
A troubadour upon the elm
Betrays the solitude.

New children play upon the green,
New weary sleep below;
And still the pensive spring returns,
And still the punctual snow!

Name: ______________________________ Date: ______________

Cyclic Patterns of Change Model

Directions: List two or three examples for each generalization.

Cycles may be constructive, destructive, or neutral.

The end of a cycle causes the cycle to begin again; a cycle may appear to have no beginning or end.

Cycles may occur naturally or may be imposed by human behavior or understanding.

Cyclic Patterns of Change

Cycles may be broken.

As repeating patterns, cycles provide structure for our passage through time.

Cycles may be added to or diminished as they contiue to repeat, forming spirals.

On the Pulse of Morning

Maya Angelou

Each new hour holds new chances
For a new beginning.
Do not be wedded forever
To fear, yoked eternally
To brutishness.

The horizon leans forward,
Offering you space
To place new steps of change
Here, on the pulse of this fine day
You may have the courage
To look up and out and upon me,
The Rock, the River, the Tree, your country.
No less to Midas than the mendicant.
No less to you now than the mastodon then.

Here, on the pulse of this new day
You may have the grace to look up and out
And into your sister's eyes,
And into your brother's face,
Your country,
And say simply
Very simply
With hope—
Good morning.

Name: ________________________________ Date: ________________

Word Sort

Directions: Cut along the lines below to make 40 small strips, each with one word. Sort the words into piles based on the similarities you see among them. Be prepared to explain why you grouped the words as you did.

COME	**COURAGE**	**AND**	**BROAD**
CLEARLY	**SING**	**TEACHER**	**NOR**
BEEN	**FIRST**	**HUMANKIND**	**ALL**
BECAUSE	**NEW**	**AHA**	**HOUR**
HIDE	**UPON**	**HOLD**	**BRIGHT**
OR	**ETERNALLY**	**HERE**	**FOR**
SIMPLY	**FOREVER**	**OH**	**SHE**
US	**THEY**	**WITH**	**TRAVELER**
BUT	**I**	**OUCH**	**YOU**
HEY	**INTO**	**OF**	**WOW**

Name: ______________________________ Date: ______________

Making Sentences

Directions: List each word from the word sort with its part of speech. Then write three sentences. Use at least one word from each part of speech in each sentence.

Nouns	Pronouns	Adjectives	Verbs

Adverbs	Prepositions	Conjunctions	Interjections

1. ______________________________

2. ______________________________

3. ______________________________

Name: ______________________________ Date: ______________

Activity 3C

Vocabulary Web

Directions: Complete the Vocabulary Web for the word *mendicant.*

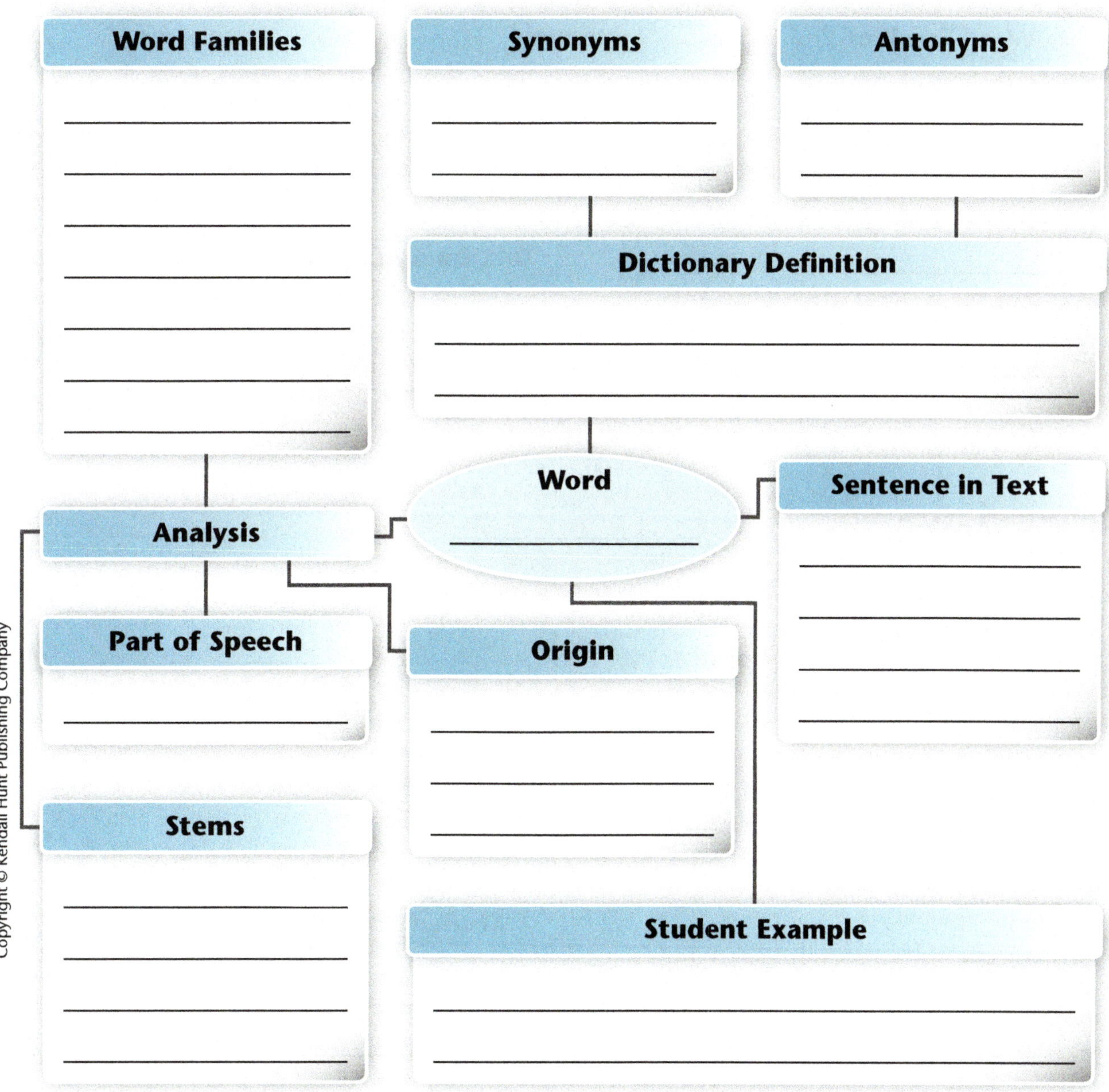

Name: ______________________ Date: ____________

Activity 3D

Vocabulary Web

Directions: Complete the Vocabulary Web for the word assigned to you.

Word Families

____
____
____
____
____
____
____

Synonyms

____
____

Antonyms

____
____

Dictionary Definition

____
____

Word

____

Sentence in Text

____
____
____
____

Analysis

Part of Speech

____

Stems

____
____
____
____

Origin

____
____
____

Student Example

____
____

The Helpful Badger

Retold by Laurence Yep

Once in Japan, there was a man named Kitabayashi. On the day that his son got married, he invited family, friends, and neighbors to a feast. There were all sorts of good things to eat, but the man made sure everyone ate some *sekiban*—a special dish of rice and red beans that was thought to bring good luck.

The guests were having such a good time that the party went on late into the night. Although there had been many people, there was still a great deal of food left over.

When the last guest had gone, Mr. Kitabayashi yawned. "It is late," he said to his wife. "Let's put everything away in the morning."

Relieved, the couple left everything where it was and went to bed. Around midnight, Mr. Kitabayashi was awakened by a noise. As he lay on his mat, he heard another thump from the next room.

Quietly, he got up and crept out into the hallway. From within the room, he heard thumps and bumps. Is it thieves? he asked himself, suddenly afraid. Slowly, he slid back a screen door and peeked inside the room.

Roaming over the floor mats were twelve creatures. Some were young; others were gray-backed elders. They waddled about on their short, stubby legs, sniffing at this or that. "Badgers! I wonder how they got in," he muttered to himself, then went to get a broom to chase them out.

When he returned, he found them all gathered around a bowl of *sekiban*. The younger ones tried to thrust their muzzles in, but the older ones rapped them sharply. Then, while the younger ones watched, the elders dipped their paws in and scooped out handfuls of *sekiban,* careful not to drop any on the floor. Mr. Kitabayashi chuckled to himself. "It's almost as if the parents are teaching the young ones manners."

Tickled, he watched the badgers eat hungrily. He noticed how thin they all looked. "Times must be hard, eh?" he whispered. "Poor badgers. Are you having trouble finding enough to eat? You must be, or why would you sneak in here?" He thought for a moment and then smiled. "I've known what it's like to be hungry. I will share our good fortune with you, for this has been a happy day."

Sliding the door shut, the kindly man put away the broom and went back to bed. "What was that noise?" his wife asked.

"Just a few guests," Mr. Kitabayashi said. "They arrived late."

"They've got some nerve," the wife said. "Did you tell them to go home?"

Mr. Kitabayashi thought of the badger family. "They'll leave soon. They've kept on their coats."

"How rude," his wife complained.

"They're not so bad," he replied. "Let's not spoil their fun." He rolled over.

However, his wife nudged him. "Well, who are they?"

"Mr. and Mrs. Badger," he mumbled sleepily.

"Badgers! In my house! They'll make a mess of everything," Mrs. Kitabayashi said, poking him urgently. "Go chase them away."

But after twenty years of marriage, Mr. Kitabayashi's back was like iron to his wife's elbow. "Not these badgers. They're very well behaved." Mr. Kitabayashi went back to sleep.

"If you aren't the oddest man," his wife said with a sigh, but she was so tired from the day that she fell asleep, too.

The next morning, the mess was exactly as they had left it—though the *sekiban* bowl had been licked completely clean. "You see," Mr. Kitabayashi said cheerfully, "I told you the badgers were polite guests."

After they had cleaned up the house, Mr. Kitabayashi went looking for a hole in the wall. When he found it, he covered it up carefully. But all the rest of the day, he felt guilty. "I wonder if the little ones are getting enough to eat?" So that evening after supper, he put out some of the leftovers outside their house.

His wife watched him, mystified. "Aren't you the strangest man? Why are you doing that?"

"It's for last night's guests," Mr. Kitabayashi said, and he told her about what he had seen.

His wife was not sure that it was such a good idea. "You'll just encourage them to come back. Badgers can be pretty rowdy animals."

"Not these badgers," Mr. Kitabayashi insisted. "They have good manners."

Since her husband was set on putting out food, Mrs. Kitabayashi stopped arguing.

The next day, all the food was gone. Mr. Kitabayashi held up the empty bowl. "You see, they did come."

"Humph, we're probably just feeding some stray cat," his wife mumbled. But that night, she let him set out more leftovers. She would have gone to bed, but Mr. Kitabayashi wanted her to stay up and see whether they came again.

"You're getting odder and odder," Mrs. Kitabayashi said in exasperation.

Her husband held onto her hand. "Perhaps, but sit with me awhile. There will be a full moon tonight. Remember how we used to sit and watch it?"

"For old time's sake, then." She pretended to grumble, but she wanted to keep an eye out inside their house.

Sure enough, as the moon rose, they watched the badgers trot toward the house with their peculiar gait. Their powerful, broad backs seemed to roll up and down. In the moonlight, their fur shone all silvery.

When the badgers encircled the bowl, they began to dip their paws in politely. "You see, it is just like I said." Mr. Kitabayashi nudged his wife.

"They're so cute," she replied.

From then on, they left food out every night. Sometimes, Mrs. Kitabayashi even made special treats for the badger family.

Then one night, Mr. Kitabayashi heard a thump inside his house. Believing that the badgers had returned, he blinked sleepily. That's gratitude for you, he thought. They've broken into our house again.

As he started to get up to scold them, the bedroom door slid to the side. Two tall shadowy figures stood in the doorway. These were no badgers.

"W-w-who are you?" stammered Mr. Kitabayashi.

Shutting the door behind them, they padded noiselessly into the room. In the moonlight, Mr. Kitabayashi saw two men. A sword blade flashed as one man drew it out. "Tell us where you have your money," the swordsman demanded.

Mr. Kitabayashi hid under the comforter and clung to his wife. "I-I-I have no money in the house."

The thief held the sword next to his throat. "Don't lie, or we'll kill you."

Suddenly, there was a loud noise in the house. The thieves

straightened and turned. "What's that?" one of them asked just as the bedroom door crashed down.

Two huge wrestlers stood in the doorway. They looked as solid as boulders with legs. One wrestler pointed toward the street for the thieves to go. Then he lifted his large hands and flexed the fingers menacingly—the robbers would face those hands if they stayed.

"You can't scare me while I have this." The swordsman raised his blade above his head and brought it down in a wicked slash. But as large as the wrestler was, he was also lightning-quick. Leaping nimbly to the side, he caught the swordsman's wrist.

With a flip and a twist, he turned the swordsman head over heels until the thief was flat on his back. Then the wrestler adjusted his grip and tightened it until the swordsman cried out in pain. When the sword clattered to the floor, the wrestler kicked it over to his partner, who picked it up.

Turning, the first wrestler glowered at the other thief. Again he pointed toward the street. Then he stamped his foot so hard that the house seemed to shake.

"Yes, whatever you say," the second thief babbled, and he helped his moaning companion to his feet. Then they dashed out of the house and were never seen again.

"You have our eternal gratitude," Mr. Kitabayashi said. He and his wife got to their knees and bowed thankfully until their foreheads touched the floor. When they straightened up, the wrestlers had vanished.

"How could anyone so big be so quiet?" Mrs. Kitabayashi asked. They looked all around the house and then out at the street, but there was no sign of their rescuers.

"Who could it be?" Mr. Kitabayashi asked his wife.

"It must have been someone magical," his wife said. "But who?"

Although they sat up for a while, trying to figure out who had rescued them, it was still a mystery. Finally, when they were both so exhausted they could not keep their eyes open, they went to sleep.

Mr. Kitabayasbi dreamed that he and his wife were sitting in their guest room in their best clothes. Then the screen door slid back and in waddled one badger after another; until they had formed a row in front of them.

At last, the largest and oldest badger stepped forward and bowed its head. "We cannot express our gratitude when you are awake. So we come in this dream to thank you. Food has been scarce of late. Without your generosity, we would have starved."

Mr. Kitabayashi was embarrassed for thinking of such intelligent creatures as pets. "Think nothing of it."

The badger raised a paw. "We would be beasts if we weren't grateful. That is why we came to your rescue."

"So it was *you* who saved us," Mr. Kitabayashi cried in delight.

"We can take many forms," the badger told him. "From now on, rest easy at night, for one of us will always be guarding you."

"And you will never go hungry," Mr. Kitabayashi promised.

"Now, in your honor, my daughters will dance," the badger said, and he sat up on his haunches. As he took a breath, his belly suddenly swelled up, and softly he began to beat time on his stomach. *"Teketen-teketen-teketen."* Then the mother joined in. *"Dokodon-dokodon-dokodon."*

One of the young ones rose on her hind legs. "We wish your family well," she said sweetly, and she did a little dance like one of the wedding guests had done. She set her hind paws down with delicate pats on the floor mats, her claws clicking in time to the drumbeat. "Pom-poko pom." She began to sing. *"Pom-poko pom."*

Another youngster leapt up and joined in. The Kitabayashis watched, fascinated, until the dance had stopped. Then with another bow, the badgers waddled out.

The next morning, Mr. Kitabayashi could not wait to tell his wife. "I just had the oddest dream." And he told her about the badgers' visit.

"Your oddness must be catching," his wife said, "because I dreamed the same thing."

That night, and every night after that, the Kitabayashis left food for the badgers. Sometimes they saw a peculiar, large rock by their front door that had not been there during the day and was gone the next morning. Then they would leave a cup of tea, for they knew it was a badger bodyguard.

Name: ______________________________ Date: ______________

Activity 4A

Literary Terms

Directions: You will complete a Vocabulary Web for one or more of these terms. During class discussion of the terms, take notes on their meaning.

antagonist ______________________________

character ______________________________

climax ______________________________

denouement ______________________________

flashback ______________________________

foreshadowing ______________________________

metaphor ______________________________

narrator/narrative voice ______________________________

plot ______________________________

protagonist ______________________________

rising action ______________________________

setting ______________________________

simile ______________________________

symbol ______________________________

theme ______________________________

tone/mood ______________________________

Name: ______________________ Date: ______________

Activity 4B

Vocabulary Web

Directions: Complete the Vocabulary Web for a literary term assigned to you.

Word Families

____
____
____
____
____
____
____

Synonyms

____
____

Antonyms

____
____

Dictionary Definition

____
____

Word

____

Sentence in Text

____
____
____
____

Analysis

Part of Speech

____

Origin

____
____
____

Stems

____
____
____
____

Student Example

____
____

Name: ______________________________ Date: ______________

Activity 4C

Vocabulary Web

Directions: Complete the Vocabulary Web for a literary term assigned to you.

Word Families

____
____
____
____
____
____
____

Synonyms

____
____

Antonyms

____
____

Dictionary Definition

____
____

Word

____

Sentence in Text

____
____
____
____

Analysis

Part of Speech

____

Origin

____
____
____

Stems

____
____
____
____

Student Example

____
____

Name: ______________________ Date: ____________

Literature Web

Directions: Complete the Literature Web for "The Helpful Badger."

Key Words

Feelings

Ideas

Title

Images/Symbols

Structure

Name: ______________________ Date: ______________

Activity 4E

Plot Map

Directions: Complete the Plot Map for "The Helpful Badger."

Rising Action 2

____
____
____
____
____
____

Climax

____
____
____
____
____
____

Rising Action 1

____
____
____
____
____
____

Denouement

____
____
____
____
____
____

Introduction

____
____
____
____

Name: ______________________________ Date: ______________

Compare and Contrast Two Folktales

Directions: Use the Venn diagram to compare and contrast "The Helpful Badger" and another folktale. Write ways they are alike in the middle part of the diagram and ways they are different in the outer parts.

"The Helpful Badger" **Both** **Another folktale**

Name: ______________________________ Date: ______________

Activity 5A

Novel Assignment

Directions: During the first half of this unit, you will read a novel of your choice and complete the following activities. Please read the requirements and record the due dates as instructed by your teacher.

Title and author of novel: ______________________________

A. Complete Literature Webs for two chapters of your choice. See Activities 5B and 5C. **Due Date:** __________

B. Keep a list of new vocabulary words from the novel in your Vocabulary Journal. Complete Vocabulary Webs for at least two words from the novel. See Activities 5D and 5E. **Due Date:** __________

C. Complete the Cycles Matrix for your novel. Include specific evidence from the novel (and page numbers for reference). You may need to use additional sheets of paper. See Activities 5F and 5G. **Due Date:** __________

D. Keep written reflections about your novel in your Literature Journal. Make an entry after about every 50 pages, or more frequently if you find something to which you particularly wish to respond. Use the following prompts to organize your writing, but you do not need to respond to every prompt in each entry. **Due Date:** Your teacher will check your Literature Journal regularly.

1. What is your reaction to what you read? Describe how you feel and why you think you feel that way.

2. Write about any experiences you have had that are similar to something that happens in the story, or about a time when you felt the way that one of the characters seems to feel.

3. Write or note an important or meaningful phrase, sentence, or passage from the reading. Explain why it seems important or meaningful to you.

4. If something in the story confuses you or brings up questions for you, write about it and try to explain why it confuses you.

5. Write about evidence in the story that supports the generalizations about cyclic patterns of change.

E. Participate in a literature circle. You will meet with other students reading your novel in order to discuss your reading.

Novel Assignment Due Date: ________

Name: ______________________________ Date: ______________

Literature Web

Directions: Complete the Literature Web for one of the chapters of the novel you are reading.

Key Words

____
____
____
____
____
____

Feelings

____
____
____
____
____
____

Ideas

____
____
____
____
____
____
____
____

Title

____
____
____
____

Images/Symbols

____
____
____
____
____
____
____
____

Structure

____
____
____
____

Name: ______________________ Date: ____________

Activity 5C

Literature Web

Directions: Complete the Literature Web for one of the chapters of the novel you are reading.

Key Words

Feelings

Ideas

Title

Images/Symbols

Structure

Name: ______________________ Date: ______________

Activity 5D

Vocabulary Web

Directions: Complete the Vocabulary Web for a word of your choice from the novel you are reading.

Word Families

____
____
____
____
____
____
____

Synonyms

____
____

Antonyms

____
____

Dictionary Definition

____
____

Word

____

Sentence in Text

____
____
____
____

Analysis

Part of Speech

____

Origin

____
____
____

Stems

____
____
____
____

Student Example

____
____

Name: ______________________________ Date: ______________

Activity 5E

Vocabulary Web

Directions: Complete the Vocabulary Web for a word of your choice from the novel you are reading.

Word Families

Synonyms

Antonyms

Dictionary Definition

Word

Sentence in Text

Analysis

Part of Speech

Origin

Stems

Student Example

Name: ______________________________ Date: ________________

Activity
5F

Cycles Matrix for Novels

Directions: Use this matrix to record ideas and examples about cycles in the novels you are reading. See Activity 5G for details about the kinds of examples to include in each column.

	Cycles in the story pattern	Cyclic imagery	Cycles and you
Your choice novel			
My Daniel			

Name: ______________________________ Date: ______________

Activity 5G

Questions for the Cycles Matrix

Directions: Think about these questions as you read your novel and work on the Cycles Matrix for Novels.

Cycles in the story pattern:

- Does the novel follow a home-away-home story pattern? If so, describe it.
- Do any of the characters "come full circle" physically, emotionally, mentally, or in terms of setting? In what way?
- Does the author use language or events in a cyclic way? Give examples.
- Is the order of events in the novel related to a cycle, such as the seasons or the days of the week? If so, describe it.

Cyclic imagery:

- Does the novel include symbols that have a cyclic shape? What are they?
- Are any symbols repeated in a cyclic way? Describe it.
- Do any metaphors, similes, or other analogies in the novel relate to cycles? Give examples.

Cycles and you:

- Did you notice any cycles in the world around you as you read this book?
- How has reading this novel helped you to understand cycles better?

Name: ______________________________ Date: ______________

Canadian Vacation

Directions: Read this sample paragraph. Think about the author's purpose and how it reflects the idea of persuasion. Circle words or groups of words that help make the writing persuasive.

Canada is a wonderful place for a vacation. It's great to go there because it's a different country. You get to learn about new customs, different money, and the French language. Canada is very big, so there are plenty of interesting things to see, including mountains, beaches, wild animals, and big cities. People in Canada are very nice. They are used to Americans, so they will help you if you are lost or confused. If you want to take a trip, try Canada. You'll have a great time!

Name: ______________________ Date: ______________

Activity 6B

Hamburger Model for Persuasive Writing

Directions: Examine and discuss the Hamburger Model for Persuasive Writing. Write each element of "Canadian Vacation" in the appropriate section of the model.

Introduction
(State your opinion.)

____

____

Elaboration	**Elaboration**	**Elaboration**
______ ______ ______	______ ______ ______	______ ______ ______
Reason	**Reason**	**Reason**
______ ______ ______	______ ______ ______	______ ______ ______
Elaboration	**Elaboration**	**Elaboration**
______ ______ ______	______ ______ ______	______ ______ ______

Conclusion

____

____

Name: ______________________________ Date: ______________

Activity 6C

Jumbled Paragraph

Directions: Cut along the dashed lines to make strips, each with one sentence. Rearrange the sentences to compose a paragraph that makes sense. Use the Hamburger Model as a guide.

If they find large fossils, they must figure out how to move them to laboratories and museums.

Therefore, although paleontology is an interesting science, it is definitely a job for strong people.

First, paleontologists spend a lot of time just trying to get money to do their work.

Paleontology is difficult work.

Often they must use forklifts and other special equipment to move the fossils.

Then they have to spend all day digging, on their knees, in hot, dry places.

Name: ______________________________ Date: ______________

Hamburger Model: Location for a Vacation

Activity 6D

Directions: Use the Hamburger Model to plan a paragraph persuading readers to visit a location of your choice. Write your paragraph on a sheet of chart paper.

Introduction (State your opinion.)

____

____

Elaboration	Elaboration	Elaboration
______ ______ ______	______ ______ ______	______ ______ ______
Reason	**Reason**	**Reason**
______ ______ ______	______ ______ ______	______ ______ ______
Elaboration	**Elaboration**	**Elaboration**
______ ______ ______	______ ______ ______	______ ______ ______

Conclusion

____

____

Name: ______________________________ Date: ______________

Activity 6E Hamburger Model: Video Games or Trick-or-Treat

Directions: Use the Hamburger Model to plan a paragraph responding to one of the following prompts: *Should students be allowed to play handheld video games at recess?* or, *Should children your age be allowed to go trick-or-treating in groups without adult supervision?* Draft your paragraph on a separate sheet of paper.

Introduction
(State your opinion.)

____

____

Elaboration	**Elaboration**	**Elaboration**
Reason	**Reason**	**Reason**
Elaboration	**Elaboration**	**Elaboration**

Conclusion

____

____

Name: ______________________________ Date: ______________

Concept Web: Generosity in "The Helpful Badger"

Directions: Examine and discuss this Concept Web. Then answer the questions.

1. What might be the purpose of this web?

____

____

2. How does its structure support its purpose?

____

____

Name: ______________________________ Date: ______________

Activity 7B

Concept Web: Hope in "On the Pulse of Morning"

Directions: Examine and discuss this Concept Web. Add your own ideas about hope in "On the Pulse of Morning" to the web.

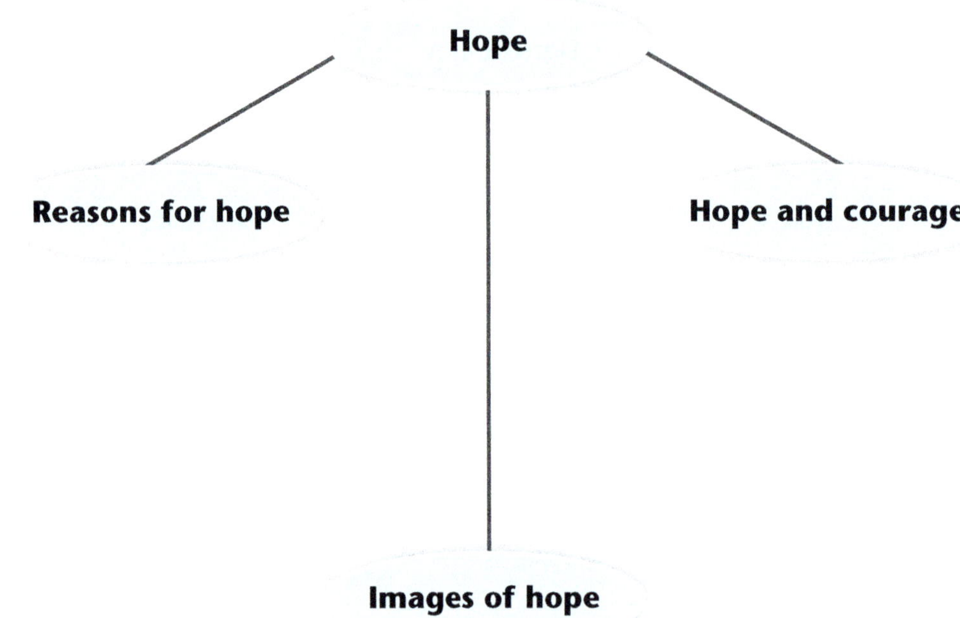

Name: ______________________________ Date: ________________

Concept Web: Gratitude in "The Helpful Badger"

Directions: Complete the Concept Web about gratitude in "The Helpful Badger." Include both generalizations about gratitude and specific examples from the story.

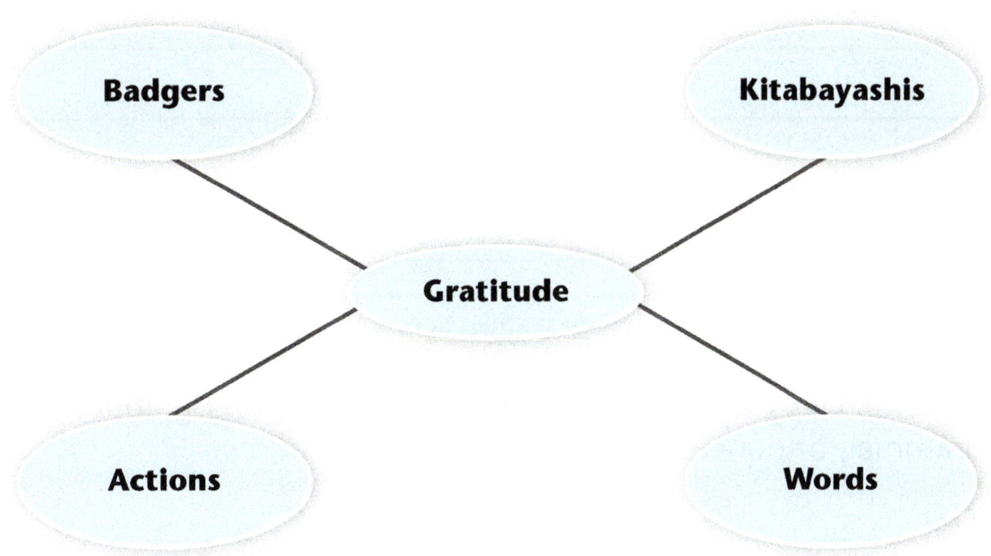

Name: ______________________________ Date: ______________

Activity 7D

Writing Process Model

Directions: Take notes about what you want to remember for each stage of the writing process. Use this summary as a guide when you write. Remember that writers do not always go through these five stages in order.

1. *Prewriting:* List your ideas and then organize them. You might use a graphic organizer such as the Hamburger Model, a web, or a Venn diagram. Later, as you write and revise, you can add to or change your graphic organizer.

Notes: ____

____

____

____

____

2. *Drafting:* Get your ideas onto paper without worrying about spelling, grammar, or punctuation.

Notes: ____

____

____

____

____

3. *Revising:* Ask other people to read and respond to your writing. Ask friends, family, or teachers to explain what they like, what they don't understand, and what they'd like to know more about. Then consider their ideas and revise your draft.

Notes: ____

____

____

____

____

4. *Editing:* Correct errors in spelling, grammar, and punctuation. Proofread your work one final time.

Notes: ____

____

____

____

____

5. *Publishing:* There are many ways to share your writing: bind your work into a book; copy it in your best handwriting or type, print, and post it on a bulletin board; read it aloud to your class or family; or make it into a gift for someone special.

Notes: ____

____

____

____

____

Name: ______________________________ Date: ______________

Activity 7E

Self-Review of Writing

Directions: Review your writing carefully. For each sentence, circle the choice that best describes your writing. Respond to the prompts.

1. My main idea is clear.

Needs improvement Satisfactory Excellent

Identify the main idea:

____

2. My details support the main idea.

Needs improvement Satisfactory Excellent

List at least three supporting details:

____

____

____

3. My ideas flow smoothly and in an orderly way.

Needs improvement Satisfactory Excellent

Underline the transitions in your essay.

4. The structure clearly follows the Hamburger Model (introduction, body, conclusion).

Needs improvement Satisfactory Excellent

Label each element of the Hamburger Model on your essay.

5. My vocabulary is rich and varied.

Needs improvement Satisfactory Excellent

List at least five strong or vivid words:

____

____

____

My writing is strong in these ways:

____

____

____

I would like help with these parts of my paragraph:

____

____

____

Name: ______________________ Date: ____________

Activity 7F

Peer Review of Writing

Writer: ______________ **Assignment:** ____________________

Directions: Read your partner's writing carefully. For each sentence, circle the choice that best describes the writing. Then complete the two sentences.

1. The main idea is clear.
   Needs improvement   Satisfactory   Excellent

2. The details support the main idea.
   Needs improvement   Satisfactory   Excellent

3. The ideas flow smoothly and in an orderly way.
   Needs improvement   Satisfactory   Excellent

4. The structure clearly follows the Hamburger Model (introduction, body, conclusion).
   Needs improvement   Satisfactory   Excellent

5. The vocabulary is rich and varied.
   Needs improvement   Satisfactory   Excellent

The writing is strong in these ways:

____

____

____

The writing could be improved in these ways:

____

____

____

Name: ______________________ Date: ______________

Concept Web: Change in a Novel

Directions: Complete the Concept Web about change in the novel you are reading. Include both generalizations about change and specific examples from the story.

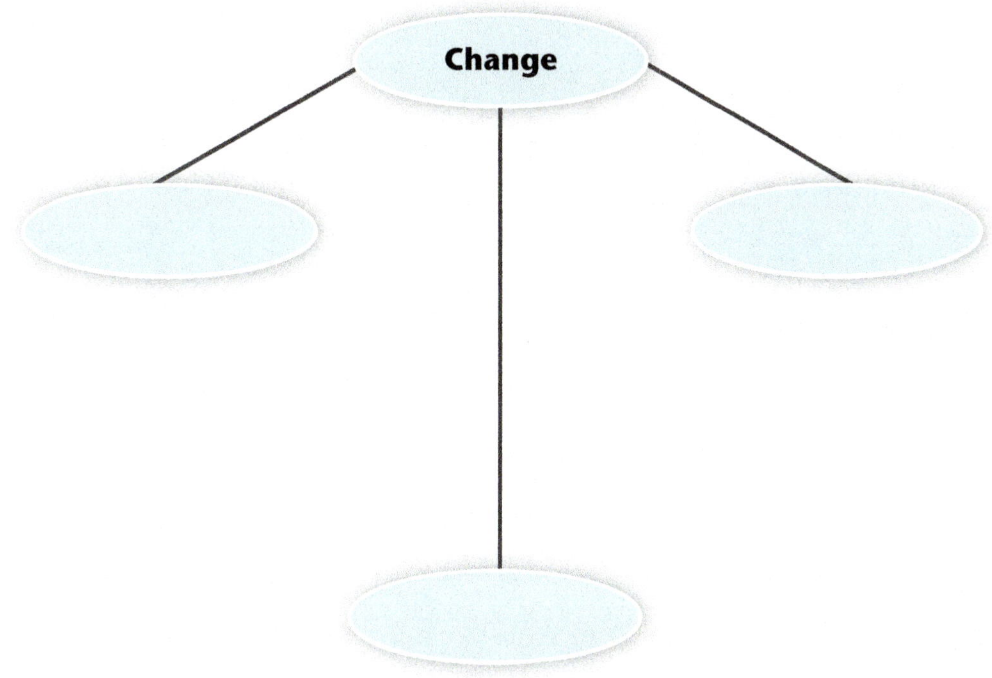

all ignorance toboggans into know

e. e. cummings

all ignorance toboggans into know
and trudges up to ignorance again:
but winter's not forever,even snow
melts;and if spring should spoil the game,what then?

all history's a winter sport or three:
but were it five,i'd still insist that all
history is too small for even me;
for me and you,exceedingly too small.

Swoop(shrill collective myth)into thy grave
   merely to toil the scale to shrillerness
per every madge and mabel dick and dave
—tomorrow is our permanent address

and there they'll scarcely find us(if they do,
we'll move away still further:into now

In the Windowsill

Mary Pleiss

Red geraniums grow in the windowsill
Night comes and they close like fans
Scented sharp and green, their crushed leaves
Perfuming the room with their own spring

Night comes, and they close like fans
The faces of children, softened by dreams
Perfuming the room with their own spring
Mud and clover and dandelion greens

The faces of children, softened by dreams
Blending their days and memories
Mud and clover and dandelion greens
Melting together in sleep and dark

Blending their days and memories
Scented sharp and green, their crushed leaves
Melting together in sleep and dark
Red geraniums grow in the windowsill

Name: ______________________ Date: ______________

Literature Web

Directions: Complete the Literature Web for "all ignorance toboggans into know" by e. e. cummings.

Key Words

____
____
____
____
____
____

Feelings

____
____
____
____
____
____

Ideas

____
____
____
____
____
____
____
____

Title

____
____
____
____

Images/Symbols

____
____
____
____
____
____
____
____

Structure

____
____
____
____

Name: ______________________________ Date: ______________

Activity 8B

Metaphor Chart

Directions: Use the chart to identify and analyze metaphors from "all ignorance toboggans into know" by e. e. cummings and other unit readings.

TOPIC of the comparison	VEHICLE (what the topic is compared to)	GROUND (characteristics the topic and vehicle share)

Name: ______________________ Date: ______________

Activity 8C

Unit Cycles Matrix

Directions: Use this matrix to record ideas and examples about cycles in the unit readings.

Reading	Cyclic Plot Patterns	Cyclic Imagery	Cyclic Themes	Cyclic Patterns in Characters'/ Speakers' Lives
Excerpt from "On the Pulse of Morning"				
"The Helpful Badger"				
"all ignorance toboggans into know"				
"In the Windowsill"				
"A Day"				

Reading	Cyclic Plot Patterns	Cyclic Imagery	Cyclic Themes	Cyclic Patterns in Characters'/ Speakers' Lives
"The Sleeping Flowers"				
"The Wind Is Blowing West"				
"A Bouquet of Wild Flowers"				
"Below"				
"Buffalo Dusk"				
"Walking"				
Sonnet II				

Name: ______________________ Date: ______________

Elements of Reasoning

Directions: Read and discuss the Elements of Reasoning.

1. *Purpose or goal:* We speak or write for a purpose. That purpose should be clear, achievable, and realistic. For example, it might be to inform, to persuade, to entertain, or to inspire.

2. *Issue or problem:* We reason to resolve an issue or question. As part of the reasoning process, we need to identify the issue to be addressed or the question to be answered.

3. *Point of view:* We must reason from a particular point of view. If the point of view is too narrow, it may be too limited or unfair. Considering other points of view may sharpen or broaden our thinking.

4. *Experiences, data, or evidence:* We must base our reasoning on experience, data, or evidence. These forms of support help to separate opinions from reasons. They need to be accurate, fair, and clear.

5. *Concepts or ideas:* All reasoning uses some ideas, principles, and rules. When we read and listen, we can ask, "What key ideas are presented?" When we write and speak, we can organize our thoughts around particular concepts and ideas.

6. *Assumptions:* We take some things for granted when we reason. We need to be aware of our own assumptions and those of others. Faulty assumptions can result in weak reasoning.

7. *Inferences or interpretations:* Reasoning proceeds by small steps of the mind called inferences. When a person concludes that something is so because of something else being so or seeming to be so, an inference has been made. We need to distinguish between our experiences and our interpretations of them (inferences). Our inferences are heavily influenced by our point of view and our assumptions.

8. *Implications and consequences:* When we argue to support a certain point of view, we must consider the possible results of following that path. The ability to reason well is measured in part by the ability to understand and identify the implications and consequences of the reasoning.

Name: ______________________________ Date: ______________

Activity 9B

Elements of Reasoning

Directions: Take notes responding to each question as your class discusses a problem.

Purpose or goal: What is the purpose of reasoning about this situation?

____

____

____

Issue or problem: What is the problem with which you are dealing?

____

____

____

Point of view: What might each of the people involved think about the problem?

____

____

____

Experiences, data, or evidence: What facts will help you make your decision?

____

____

____

Concepts or ideas: What big ideas are involved in this problem?

Assumptions: What assumptions might you or other people make?

Inferences: What are some inferences or small conclusions that you can make based on the facts you have?

Implications and consequences: What might be the outcome of either decision you could make?

Name: ______________________________ Date: ______________

I Should Have a Later Bedtime

Directions: Read the paragraph and think about how the writer uses the Elements of Reasoning.

I should be allowed to stay up half an hour later than I do right now. I'm a year older than I was when you set my bedtime. I can stay awake longer than I used to, and most of the time I read for that long before I fall asleep anyway. Another reason that I need to stay up later is that I have more homework now than I used to. With a little more time, I can finish the homework and still be able to relax and play for a while before I have to go to bed. Finally, I would be more pleasant to be around if I could stay up later. I wouldn't complain about the sun still being up, and I wouldn't be constantly bugging you to let me stay up "just a little while longer" the way I do right now. Therefore, so we can all be happier and more productive, I think you should extend my bedtime by half an hour.

Name: ____________________ Date: ____________

Activity 9D

Hamburger Model: Later Bedtime

Directions: Identify the elements of the paragraph "I Should Have a Later Bedtime" that belong in each part of the Hamburger Model. Write each element of the paragraph, including the introduction, reasons, elaboration, and conclusion, in the appropriate part of the model.

Introduction (State your opinion.)

____

____

Elaboration	**Elaboration**	**Elaboration**
____________	____________	____________
Reason	**Reason**	**Reason**
____________	____________	____________
Elaboration	**Elaboration**	**Elaboration**
____________	____________	____________

Conclusion

____

____

Name: ______________________________ Date: ______________

Activity 9E

Standards of Reasoning

Directions: Evaluate the argument in "I Should Have a Later Bedtime" by responding to the questions.

Are enough reasons given to make the argument convincing? Explain your answer.

____

____

____

____

Is the supporting evidence factual and correct? Give an example that supports your response.

____

____

____

____

Are the reasons clear? Are they explained thoroughly, or is more information needed? Give an example that supports your response.

____

____

____

____

Are the reasons and evidence specific, or are they general and vague? Give an example that supports your response.

Are the reasons strong and important, or do they seem to be included just so that the author has something to say? Give an example that supports your response.

Is the argument logical? Do the sentences seem to go together, and does their sequence make sense? Or does the paragraph sound like a set of disconnected statements? Give an example that supports your response.

Name: ______________________________ Date: ______________

Hamburger Model: Afternoon Snack

Activity 9F

Directions: Use the Hamburger Model to plan a letter to the editor of your school paper about the following issue: *Should all students be allowed to have an afternoon snack? Why or why not?* Draft your letter on a separate sheet of paper.

Introduction (State your opinion.)

____

____

Elaboration	**Elaboration**	**Elaboration**
______________	______________	______________
______________	______________	______________
Reason	**Reason**	**Reason**
______________	______________	______________
______________	______________	______________
Elaboration	**Elaboration**	**Elaboration**
______________	______________	______________
______________	______________	______________

Conclusion

____

____

A Day

Emily Dickinson

I'll tell you how the sun rose, —
A ribbon at a time.
The steeples swam in amethyst,
The news like squirrels ran.
The hills untied their bonnets,
The bobolinks begun.
Then I said softly to myself,
"That must have been the sun!"

But how he set, I know not.
There seemed a purple stile
Which little yellow boys and girls
Were climbing all the while
Till when they reached the other side,
A dominie in gray
Put gently up the evening bars,
And led the flock away.

The Sleeping Flowers

Emily Dickinson

"Whose are the little beds," I asked,
"Which in the valleys lie?"
Some shook their heads, and others smiled,
And no one made reply.
"Perhaps they did not hear," I said;
"I will inquire again.
Whose are the beds, the tiny beds
So thick upon the plain?"
"'T is daisy in the shortest;
A little farther on,
Nearest the door to wake the first,
Little leontodon.
"'T is iris, sir, and aster,
Anemone and bell,
Batschia in the blanket red,
And chubby daffodil."
Meanwhile at many cradles
Her busy foot she plied,
Humming the quaintest lullaby
That ever rocked a child.
"Hush! Epigea wakens! —
The crocus stirs her lids,
Rhodora's cheek is crimson, —
She's dreaming of the woods."
Then, turning from them, reverent,
"Their bed-time 't is," she said;
"The bumble-bees will wake them
When April woods are red."

The Wind Is Blowing West

Joseph Ceravolo

1
I am trying to decide to go swimming,
But the sea looks so calm.
All the other boys have gone in.
I can't decide what to do.

I've been waiting in my tent
Expecting to go in.
Have you forgotten to come down?
Can I escape going in?
I was just coming

I was just going in
But lost my pail

2
A boisterous tide is coming up;
I was just looking at it.
The pail is near me
again. My shoulders have sand on them.

Round the edge of the tide
Is the shore. The shore
Is filled with waves.
They are tin waves.

Boisterous tide coming up.
The tide is getting less.

3
Daytime is not a brain,
Living is not a cricket's song.
Why does light diffuse
As earth turns away from the sun?

I want to give my food
To a stranger. I want
to be taken.
What kind of a face do

I have while leaving?
I'm thinking of my friend.

4
I am trying to go swimming
But the sea looks so calm
All boys are gone
I can't decide what to do

I've been waiting to go
Have you come down?
Can I escape

I am just coming
    Just going in

Name: ______________________ Date: ______________

Literature Web

Directions: Complete the Literature Web for your poem.

Key Words

Feelings

Ideas

Title

Images/Symbols

Structure

Name: ______________________________ Date: ______________

Activity 10B

Poetry Comparison Chart

Directions: Complete the chart with notes about the poems.

Title	"A Day" and "The Sleeping Flowers"	"The Wind Is Blowing West"
Poet		
Approximate date you think the poem(s) was/were written (include evidence)		
Structure		
Author's style		
Symbols used and what they represent		
Significant words and phrases		
Theme		
Cycles represented in the poem(s)		

Name: ______________________________ Date: ________________

Compare and Contrast Poems by Dickinson and Ceravolo

Directions: Complete the Venn diagram with similarities and differences between the poems by Dickinson and "The Wind Is Blowing West." Use your notes on Activity 10B to help you.

Poems by Dickinson	**Both**	**"The Wind Is Blowing West"**

Name: ________________________________ Date: ________________

Activity 10D

Vocabulary Web

Directions: Complete the Vocabulary Web for the word assigned to you.

Word Families

____
____
____
____
____
____
____

Synonyms

____
____

Antonyms

____
____

Dictionary Definition

____
____

Word

____

Sentence in Text

____
____
____
____

Analysis

Part of Speech

____

Origin

____
____
____

Stems

____
____
____
____

Student Example

____
____

Name: ________________________________ Date: ________________

Hamburger Model: Cyclic Patterns in Poetry

Activity 10E

Directions: Use the Hamburger Model to plan a persuasive paragraph explaining which poem you think best illustrates one of the generalizations about cyclic patterns of change: "A Day" or "The Sleeping Flowers" by Emily Dickinson, or "The Wind Is Blowing West" by Joseph Ceravolo.

Introduction
(State your opinion.)

____

____

Elaboration	**Elaboration**	**Elaboration**
____________ ____________	____________ ____________	____________ ____________
Reason	**Reason**	**Reason**
____________ ____________	____________ ____________	____________ ____________
Elaboration	**Elaboration**	**Elaboration**
____________ ____________	____________ ____________	____________ ____________

Conclusion

____

____

Name: ______________________ Date: ____________

Activity 11A

Wheel of Reasoning

Directions: Refer to the Wheel of Reasoning as you discuss an article.

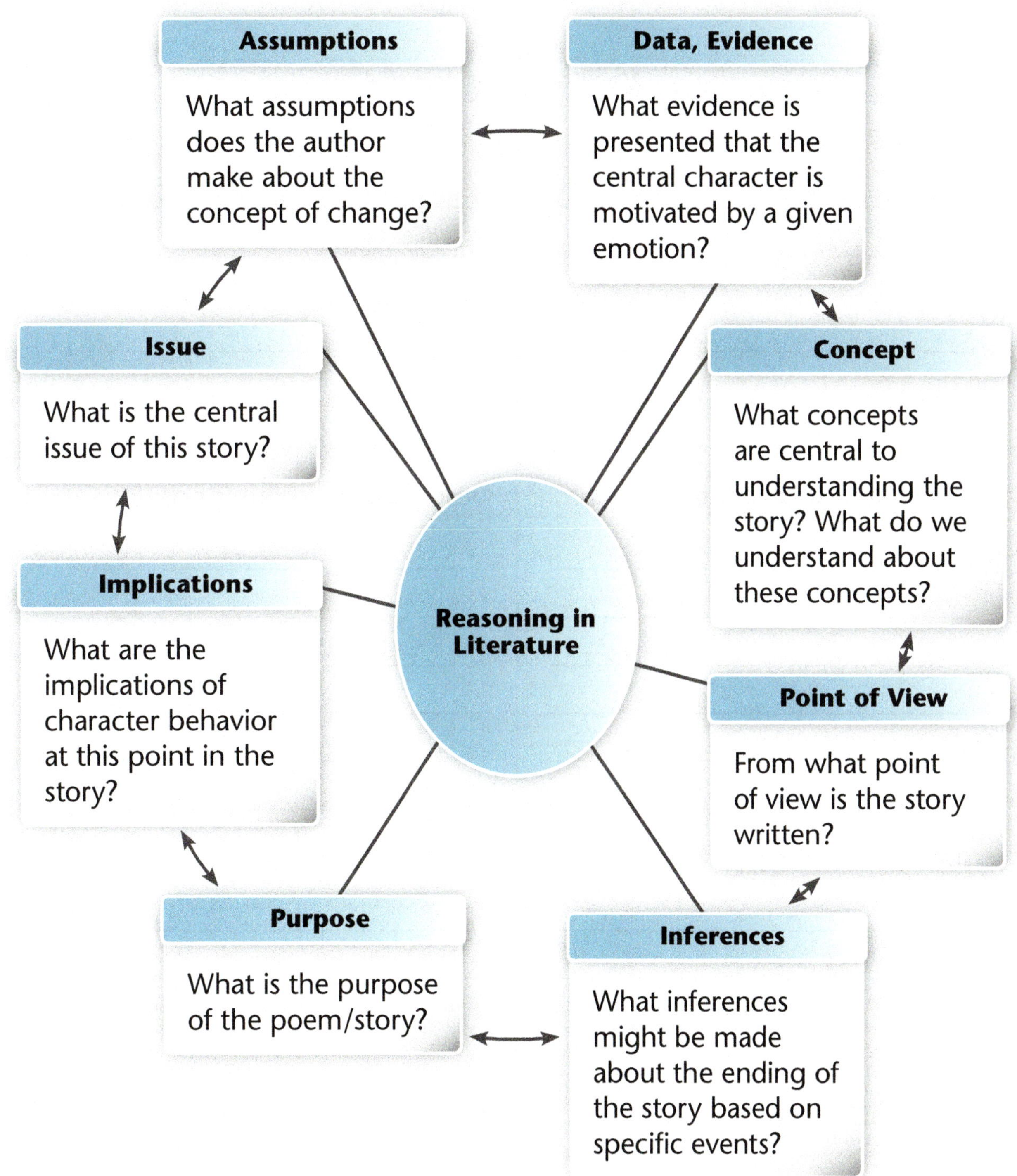

Name: ______________________ Date: ______________

Activity 11B

Developing an Issue

Directions: First, state the issue. Next, identify the stakeholder groups and their positions. Finally, state your own point of view about the issue.

Developing an Issue	
State the issue:	
Identify the stakeholder groups:	Describe each group's position:
State your initial position:	

Name: ______________________ Date: ______________

Research Model Planner

Activity 11C

Directions: Use this planner to guide you as you research your issue. Use your own paper to record your responses so that you have enough space for all your ideas.

1. Identify your issue or problem.

- What is the issue or problem?

____

____

____

- Who are the stakeholders and what are their positions?

____

____

____

- What is my position on this issue?

____

____

____

2. Read about your issue and identify points of view or arguments through information sources.

- What are my print sources?

___

___

___

- What are my media sources?

___

___

___

- What are my people sources?

___

___

___

- What primary and secondary source documents might I use?

___

___

___

- What are my preliminary findings based on a review of existing sources?

___

___

___

3. Form a set of questions that can be answered by a specific set of data:

- What would be the results of ________________________________?
- Who would benefit and by how much?

____

____

____

- Who would be harmed and by how much?

____

____

____

- My research questions:

____

____

____

4. Gather evidence through research techniques such as surveys, interviews, or analysis of primary and secondary source documents.

- What survey questions should I ask?

____

____

____

- What interview questions should I ask?

- What generalizations do secondary sources give?

- What data and evidence can I find in primary sources to support different sides of the issue?

5. Manipulate and transform data so that they can be interpreted.

- How can I summarize what I learned?

- Should I develop charts, diagrams, or graphs to represent my data?

6. Draw conclusions and make inferences.

- What do the data mean? How can I interpret what I found out?

- How do the data support my original point of view?

- How do they support other points of view?

- What conclusions can I make about the issue?

- What is my point of view now, based on the data?

7. Determine implications and consequences.

   - What are the consequences of following the point of view that I support?

   ____

   ____

   ____

   - Do I know enough or are there now new questions to be answered?

   ____

   ____

   ____

8. Communicate your findings. (Prepare a paper and oral presentation.)

   - What are my purpose, issue, and point of view, and how will I explain them?

   ____

   ____

   ____

   - What data will I use to support my point of view?

   ____

   ____

   ____

   - How will I conclude my presentation?

   ____

   ____

   ____

Name: ______________________ Date: ______________

Activity 11D

Topic Web

Directions: Use this web to plan the information-gathering process for the unit research project.

What do I want to know? (List questions.)

What information resources would be best to explore for each question?

Topic

What did I find out from each source?

What did I learn?

Name: ________________________________ Date: ________________

Developing an Issue for Research

Directions: Complete the chart for your issue for research.

Developing an Issue	
State the issue: ______ ______ ______ ______ ______ ______	
Identify the stakeholder groups: ______ ______ ______ ______ ______ ______	Describe each group's position: ______ ______ ______ ______ ______ ______
State your initial position: ______ ______ ______ ______ ______	

Name: ______________________________ Date: ______________

Getting to Know the Author

Directions: Use this page to take notes as you gather information about the author of the novel you read.

Author: ______________________________

Date and place of birth: ______________________________

Childhood experiences:

____

____

____

____

____

____

____

Other interesting experiences and interests:

____

____

____

____

____

____

____

Reasons for writing novels:

Other books and awards:

Sources of information:

Name: ______________________________ Date: ______________

Symbols for Myself

Directions: Complete the following sentences. On each line, write a specific example of the general noun given below the line. For example, a cat is a specific example of an animal. Choose a specific example that reflects your personality or behavior. Following the word *because,* explain why this example fits you well.

1. I am like a(n) ______________ because
animal

____

____

____

____

2. I am like ______________ because
color

____

____

____

____

3. I am like ______________ because
number

____

____

____

____

4. I am like ____________________ because
type or piece of music

____

____

____

____

5. I am like ____________________ because
type of weather

____

____

____

____

6. I am like ____________________ because
any object of your choice

____

____

____

____

Name: ______________________ Date: ______________

Relationships Chart

Directions: Write the name of the protagonist in the novel you read as the title of the chart. Write the names of the other important characters in the first column. For each character, draw or write at least one symbol that represents the protagonist's relationship with that character. Draw or write each symbol in the appropriate column.

Protagonist: ______________________

Character	Animal	Color	Number	Type or Piece of Music	Type of Weather	Another Object

Name: ______________________________________ Date: __________________

Activity 13C

Character Mandala

Directions: Create a mandala showing symbols that represent relationships between the protagonist of the novel you read and the other characters. In the center of the mandala, write the name of the protagonist. In the other sections, write the name of a character and sketch or write a symbol or symbols representing the relationship between the protagonist and that character.

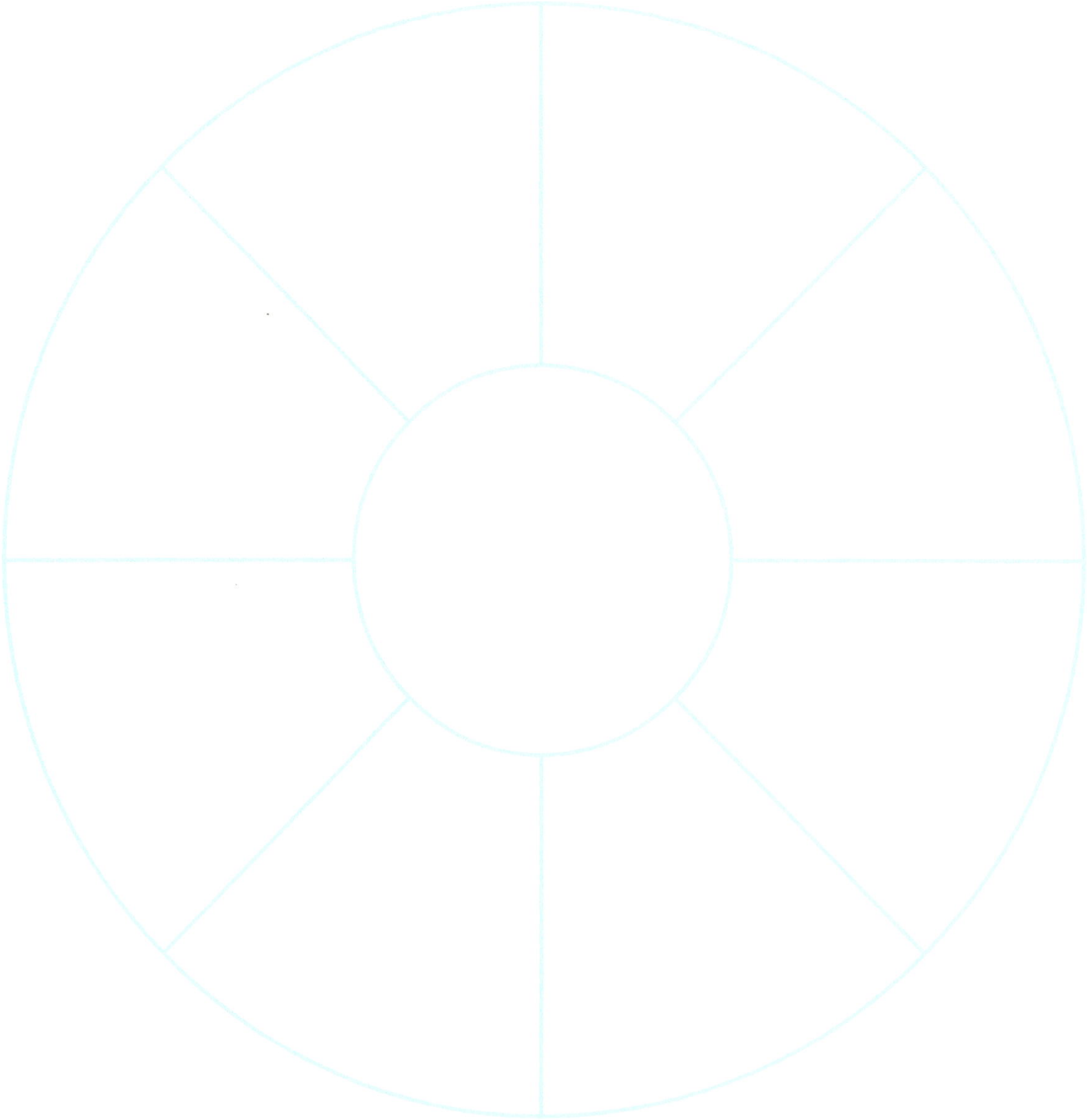

Name: ______________________ Date: ______________

Activity 13D

Relationships Chart

Directions: Write the names of three people you know well in the first column of the chart. For each person, draw or write at least one symbol that represents your relationship with that person. Draw or write each symbol in the appropriate column. Then explain each choice on the following page.

Person	Animal	Color	Number	Type or Piece of Music	Type of Weather	Another Object
1.						
2.						
3.						

3. Develop an introduction for your essay that responds to your question by stating a **point of view** about this decision and the way it influenced the characters and events in your novel.

What is your point of view about this decision?

____

____

____

____

____

4. Develop at least **three reasons** to support your opinion, and elaborate upon each. Use examples, evidence, and quotes from the novel for elaboration, as well as figurative language, such as metaphors and similes, to illustrate your points. Try to focus on what *might* have happened (implications of a different decision), as well as what actually *did* happen when evaluating the character's decision.

What reasons support your opinion?

____

____

____

____

____

5. Develop a **conclusion** for your essay that revisits your main ideas.

____

____

____

____

Name: ______________________ Date: ______________

Hamburger Model: The Big Decision

Activity 14B

Directions: Use the Hamburger Model to organize your ideas for an essay about a decision made by a character in the novel you read. Refer to Student Activity Page 14A, your Literature Journal entries, and Literature Webs for the novel as needed.

Introduction (State your opinion.)

____

____

Elaboration	**Elaboration**	**Elaboration**
______	______	______
Reason	**Reason**	**Reason**
______	______	______
Elaboration	**Elaboration**	**Elaboration**
______	______	______

Conclusion

____

____

Name: ______________________________ Date: ______________

Activity 14C

Peer Review of Writing

Writer: ________________ **Assignment:** ______________________

Directions: Read your partner's writing carefully. For each sentence, circle the choice that best describes the writing. Then complete the two sentences.

1. The main idea is clear.

   Needs improvement Satisfactory Excellent

Identify the main idea:

____

2. The details support the main idea.

   Needs improvement Satisfactory Excellent

List at least three supporting details:

____

____

____

3. The ideas flow smoothly and in an orderly way.

   Needs improvement Satisfactory Excellent

Underline the transitions in the essay.

4. The structure clearly follows the Hamburger Model (introduction, body, conclusion).

   Needs improvement Satisfactory Excellent

Label each element of the Hamburger Model on your essay.

5. The vocabulary is rich and varied.

Needs improvement   Satisfactory   Excellent

List at least five strong or vivid words:

______

______

______

The writing is strong in these ways:

______

______

______

The writing could be improved in these ways:

______

______

______

Name: ______________________________ Date: ______________

Activity 14D
Standards of Reasoning

Directions: Evaluate the argument in your partner's essay by responding to the questions.

Are enough reasons given to make the argument convincing? Explain your answer.

____

____

____

____

Is the supporting evidence factual and correct? Give an example that supports your response.

____

____

____

____

Are the reasons clear? Are they explained thoroughly, or is more information needed? Give an example that supports your response.

____

____

____

____

Are the reasons and evidence specific, or are they general and vague? Give an example that supports your response.

___

___

___

___

Are the reasons strong and important, or do they seem to be included just so that the author has something to say? Give an example that supports your response.

___

___

___

___

Is the argument logical? Do the sentences seem to go together, and does their sequence make sense? Or does the paragraph sound like a set of disconnected statements? Give an example that supports your response.

___

___

___

___

Name: ______________________ Date: ______________

Activity 14E

Self-Review of Writing

Directions: Review your writing carefully. For each sentence, circle the choice that best describes your writing. Respond to the prompts.

1. My main idea is clear.

   Needs improvement   Satisfactory   Excellent

Identify the main idea:

____

2. My details support the main idea.

   Needs improvement   Satisfactory   Excellent

List at least three supporting details:

____

____

____

3. My ideas flow smoothly and in an orderly way.

   Needs improvement   Satisfactory   Excellent

Underline the transitions in your essay.

4. The structure clearly follows the Hamburger Model (introduction, body, conclusion).

   Needs improvement   Satisfactory   Excellent

Label each element of the Hamburger Model on your essay.

5. My vocabulary is rich and varied.

Needs improvement Satisfactory Excellent

List at least five strong or vivid words:

____

____

____

My writing is strong in these ways:

____

____

____

I would like help with these parts of my paragraph:

____

____

____

A Bouquet of Wild Flowers

Laura Ingalls Wilder

The Man of the Place brought me a bouquet of wild flowers this morning. It has been a habit of his for years. He never brings me cultivated flowers but always the wild blossoms of field and woodland, and I think them much more beautiful.

In my bouquet this morning was a purple flag. Do you remember gathering them down on the flats and in the creek bottoms when you were a barefoot child? There was one marshy corner of the pasture down by the creek, where the grass grew lush and green; where the cows loved to feed and could always be found when it was time to drive them up at night. All thru the tall grass were scattered purple and white flag blossoms and I have stood in that peaceful grassland corner, with the red cow and the spotted cow and the roan taking their goodnight mouthfuls of the sweet grass, and watched the sun setting behind the hilltop and loved the purple flags and the rippling brook and wondered at the beauty of the world, while I wriggled my bare toes down into the soft grass.

The wild Sweet Williams in my bouquet brought a far different picture to my mind. A window had been broken in the schoolhouse at the country crossroads and the pieces of glass lay scattered where they had fallen. Several little girls going to school for their first term had picked handfuls of Sweet Williams and were gathered near the window. Someone discovered that the blossoms could be pulled from the stem and, by wetting their faces, could be stuck to the pieces of glass in whatever fashion they were arranged. They dried on the glass and would stay that way for hours and, looked at thru

Originally appeared in the *Missouri Realist,* July 20, 1917.

the glass, were very pretty. I was one of those little girls and tho I have forgotten what it was that I tried to learn out of a book that summer, I never have forgotten the beautiful wreaths and stars and other figures we made on the glass with the Sweet Williams. The delicate fragrance of their blossoms this morning made me feel like a little girl again.

The little white daisies with their hearts of gold grew thickly along the path where we walked to Sunday school. Father and sister and I used to walk the 2 ½ miles every Sunday morning. The horses had worked hard all the week and must rest this one day, and Mother would rather stay at home with baby brother, so with Father and Sister Mary I walked to the church thru the beauties of the sunny spring Sundays. I have forgotten what I was taught on those days also. I was only a little girl, you know. But I can still plainly see the grass and the trees and the path winding ahead, flecked with sunshine and shadow and the beautiful golden-hearted daisies scattered all along the way.

Ah well! That was years ago and there have been so many changes since then that it would seem such simple things should be forgotten, but at the long last, I am beginning to learn that it is the sweet, simple things of life which are the real ones after all.

We heap up around us things that we do not need as the crow makes piles of glittering pebbles. We gabble words like parrots until we lose the sense of their meaning; we chase after this new idea and that; we take an old thought and dress it out in so many words that the thought itself is lost in its clothing like a slim woman in a barrel skirt and then we exclaim, "Lo, the wonderful new thought I have found!"

"There is nothing new under the sun," says the proverb. I think the meaning is that there are just so many truths or laws of life and no matter how far we may think we have advanced we cannot get beyond those laws. However complex a structure we build of living we must come back to those truths and so we find we have traveled in a circle.

The Russian revolution has only taken the Russian people back to the democratic form of government they had at the beginning of history in medieval times and so a republic is nothing new. I believe we would be happier to have a personal revolution in our individual lives and go back to simpler living and more direct thinking. It is the simple things of life that make living worth while, the sweet fundamental things such as love and duty, work and rest and living close to nature. There are no hothouse blossoms that can compare in beauty and fragrance with my bouquet of wild flowers.

Name: ______________________ Date: ______________

Activity 15A

Literature Web

Directions: Complete the Literature Web for "A Bouquet of Wild Flowers."

Key Words

Feelings

Ideas

Title

Images/Symbols

Structure

Name: ______________________________ Date: ______________

Symbolic Meanings of Flowers

Directions: People have associated certain flowers with specific meanings for hundreds of years. In the Victorian era (1837–1901), people would send bouquets as messages, declaring love, friendship, rejection, appreciation, and many other feelings. The chart shows the meanings given to some popular plants and flowers. Keep these meanings in mind when selecting flowers for your memory wreath.

Plant or Flower	Meaning
Aloe	Wisdom and integrity
Baby's Breath	Happiness
Cactus	Bravery and endurance
Carnation (red)	Admiration
Daisy	Gentleness and innocence
Dandelion	Time and love
Fern	Sincerity
Geranium	Affection and friendship
Holly	Foresight, good planning, or prediction
Iris	Faith, wisdom, valor
Ivy	Friendship
Marigold	Affection
Pansy	Thoughts
Rose (red)	True love
Rose (yellow)	Friendship
Snapdragon	No, refusal
Sunflower	Devotion
Tulip	Perfect love
Violet	Modesty and simplicity
Water Lily	Persuasion

Name: ______________________ Date: ____________

Activity 15C

Vocabulary Web

Directions: Complete the Vocabulary Web for one of the following words: *cultivated, proverb, republic,* or *fundamental.*

Word Families

Synonyms

Antonyms

Dictionary Definition

Word

Sentence in Text

Analysis

Part of Speech

Origin

Stems

Student Example

Name: ______________________________ Date: ______________

Activity 15D

Vocabulary Web

Directions: Complete the Vocabulary Web for another of the following words: *cultivated, proverb, republic,* or *fundamental.*

Word Families

____
____
____
____
____
____
____

Synonyms

____
____

Antonyms

____
____

Dictionary Definition

____
____

Word

____

Analysis

Sentence in Text

____
____
____
____

Part of Speech

____

Origin

____
____
____

Stems

____
____
____
____

Student Example

____
____

Name: ______________________________ Date: ______________

Activity 16A

Persuasion Chart

Directions: List and analyze examples of past attempts at persuasion by answering the questions on this chart.

WHO: Who was your audience?	**WHAT:** What was the issue you were addressing?	**HOW:** What arguments did you use?	**RESULTS:** How successful were you in persuading your audience?

Name: ______________________________ Date: ______________

Activity 16B

Oral Presentation Evaluation Form

Speaker: ______________ **Assignment:** ____________________

Directions: For 1–8, circle the choice that describes the presentation. Then complete the two sentences.

Content and Organization

1. The purpose of the presentation was clear.
   Needs improvement   Satisfactory   Excellent

2. The speaker included details that supported the main idea.
   Needs improvement   Satisfactory   Excellent

3. The speaker addressed opposing points of view.
   Needs improvement   Satisfactory   Excellent

4. The speaker showed knowledge of the subject.
   Needs improvement   Satisfactory   Excellent

5. The speaker closed the presentation with a strong, interesting idea that restated the purpose.
   Needs improvement   Satisfactory   Excellent

Delivery

6. The speaker made good eye contact with the audience.
   Needs improvement   Satisfactory   Excellent

7. The speaker spoke loudly enough for the entire audience to hear.
   Needs improvement   Satisfactory   Excellent

8. The speaker's words were clear and could be understood.
   Needs improvement   Satisfactory   Excellent

The best part of this presentation was:

____

____

____

____

A suggestion for improvement is:

____

____

____

____

Name: ______________________ Date: ______________

Activity 16C

Oral Presentation Evaluation Form

Speaker: ______________ **Assignment:** ______________________

Directions: For 1–8, circle the choice that describes the speech. Then complete the two sentences.

Content and Organization

1. The purpose of the speech was clear.
   Needs improvement Satisfactory Excellent

2. The speaker included details that supported the main idea.
   Needs improvement Satisfactory Excellent

3. The speaker addressed opposing points of view.
   Needs improvement Satisfactory Excellent

4. The speaker showed knowledge of the subject.
   Needs improvement Satisfactory Excellent

5. The speaker closed the speech with a strong, interesting idea that restated the purpose.
   Needs improvement Satisfactory Excellent

Delivery

6. The speaker made good eye contact with the audience.
   Needs improvement Satisfactory Excellent

7. The speaker spoke loudly enough for the entire audience to hear.
   Needs improvement Satisfactory Excellent

8. The speaker's words were clear and could be understood.
   Needs improvement Satisfactory Excellent

The best part of this speech was:

A suggestion for improvement is:

Buffalo Dusk

Carl Sandburg

The buffaloes are gone.
And those who saw the buffaloes are gone.
Those who saw the buffaloes by thousands and how they pawed the
prairie sod into dust with their hoofs, their great heads down
pawing on in a great pageant of dusk,
Those who saw the buffaloes are gone.
And the buffaloes are gone.

From *Smoke and Steel,* 1920, Harcourt Brace.

Below

Joseph Bruchac

A Hopi friend
once told me that the people came
from another world beneath this world. Before that world,
they lived in another and
another one still, so that the world
we live in today is the fourth one
the people have known.

Each time, it seems,
things were going well,
until something happened
that made things go wrong.
People acted jealous,
people fought one another.
People didn't remember to respect the sacred.
Coyote caused the greatest trouble,
when he stole the child of the water monster.
When the water monster took back its child,
the whole third world was washed over by flood.

So the people left their old world behind.
They had to climb higher
to another, safer place.

"Below" from *Between Earth and Sky, Legends of Native American Sacred Places,* copyright © 1996 by Joseph Bruchac. Reprinted by permission of Harcourt. Inc.

Perhaps that great canyon
in the heart of their lands
was meant to remind us
of those worlds that were lost
before we reached this rainbow world
no one wants to leave behind.

Name: ______________________ Date: ____________

Activity 17A

Literature Web

Directions: Complete the Literature Web for "Buffalo Dusk."

Key Words

Feelings

Ideas

Title

Images/Symbols

Structure

Name: ______________________ Date: ______________

Activity 17B

Literature Web

Directions: Complete the Literature Web for "Below."

Key Words

Feelings

Ideas

Title

Images/Symbols

Structure

Name: ______________________________ Date: ______________

Activity 17C Novel Assignment: *My Daniel*

Directions: During the second half of this unit, you will read the novel *My Daniel* by Pam Conrad and complete the following activities. Please read the requirements and fill in the due dates as instructed by your teacher.

A. Complete Literature Webs for two chapters of your choice. See Activities 17D and 17E. **Due Date:** __________

B. Complete one of the following activities. **Due Date:** __________

EITHER

- Create a graphic organizer that represents the relationships between important characters. You may use a mandala or some other creative graphic representation.

OR

- Create a Plot Map, using images and words to show events in the story's settings.

C. Keep a list of new vocabulary words from the novel in your Vocabulary Journal. Record the definition of each word and the sentence in which you encountered it. Complete Vocabulary Webs for at least three of the words. See Activities 17F, 17G, and 17H. **Due Date:** __________

D. Complete the Cycles Matrix for *My Daniel.* Include specific evidence from the novel (and page numbers for reference). You may need to use additional sheets of paper. See Activities 5F and 5G.
Due Date: __________

E. Keep written reflections about your novel in your Literature Journal. Make an entry after you read Chapter 4, Chapter 7, Chapter 11, and Chapter 15, or more frequently if you find something to which you particularly wish to respond. Use the following prompts to organize your writing, but you do not need to respond to every prompt in each entry. **Due Date:** Your teacher will check your Literature Journal regularly.

1. What is your reaction to what you read? Describe how you feel and why you think you feel that way.

2. Write about any experiences you have had that are similar to something that happens in the story, or about a time when you felt the way that one of the characters seems to feel.

3. Write or note an important or meaningful phrase, sentence, or passage from the reading. Explain why it seems important or meaningful to you.

4. If something in the story confuses you or brings up questions for you, write about it and try to explain why it confuses you.

5. Note evidence of cyclic patterns of change in the characters, plot, or setting of the story. Write about evidence in the story that supports the generalizations about cyclic patterns of change.

Novel Assignment Due Date: __________

Name: ______________________ Date: ______________

Activity 17D

Literature Web

Directions: Complete the Literature Web for one of the chapters of *My Daniel.*

Key Words

____
____
____
____
____
____

Feelings

____
____
____
____
____
____

Ideas

____
____
____
____
____
____
____
____

Title

____
____
____
____

Images/Symbols

____
____
____
____
____
____
____
____

Structure

____
____
____
____

Name: ______________________ Date: ______________

Literature Web

Directions: Complete the Literature Web for one of the chapters of *My Daniel.*

Key Words

____
____
____
____
____
____

Feelings

____
____
____
____
____
____

Ideas

____
____
____
____
____
____
____
____

Title

____
____
____
____

Images/Symbols

____
____
____
____
____
____
____
____

Structure

____
____
____
____

Name: ______________________ Date: ______________

Activity 17F

Vocabulary Web

Directions: Complete the Vocabulary Web for a word of your choice from *My Daniel.*

Word Families

Synonyms

Antonyms

Dictionary Definition

Word

Analysis

Sentence in Text

Part of Speech

Origin

Stems

Student Example

Name: ______________________ Date: ______________

Activity 17G

Vocabulary Web

Directions: Complete the Vocabulary Web for a word of your choice from *My Daniel.*

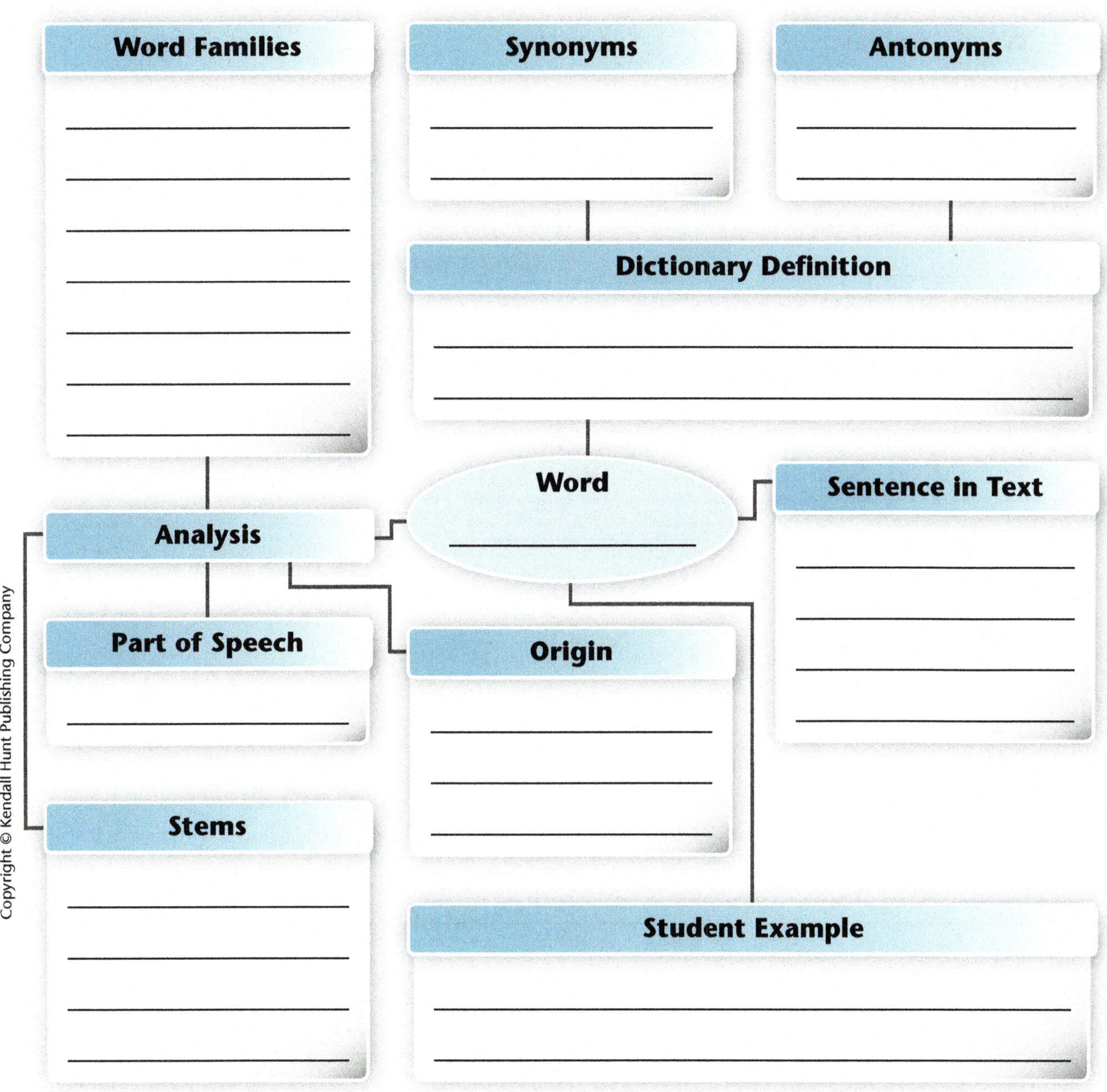

Name: ______________________________ Date: ______________

Activity 17H

Vocabulary Web

Directions: Complete the Vocabulary Web for a word of your choice from *My Daniel.*

Word Families

Synonyms

Antonyms

Dictionary Definition

Word

Sentence in Text

Analysis

Part of Speech

Origin

Stems

Student Example

Name: ______________________________ Date: ______________

Self-Review of Writing

Directions: Review your writing carefully. For each sentence, circle the choice that best describes your writing. Respond to the prompts.

1. My main idea is clear.

   Needs improvement   Satisfactory   Excellent

Identify the main idea:

____

2. My details support the main idea.

   Needs improvement   Satisfactory   Excellent

List at least three supporting details:

____

____

____

3. My ideas flow smoothly and in an orderly way.

   Needs improvement   Satisfactory   Excellent

Underline the transitions in your essay.

4. The structure clearly follows the Hamburger Model (introduction, body, conclusion).

   Needs improvement   Satisfactory   Excellent

Label each element of the Hamburger Model on your essay.

5. My vocabulary is rich and varied.

Needs improvement Satisfactory Excellent

List at least five strong or vivid words:

____

____

____

My writing is strong in these ways:

____

____

____

I would like help with these parts of my paragraph:

____

____

____

Name: ______________________________ Date: ______________

Peer Review of Writing

Writer: ________________ **Assignment:** ______________________

Directions: Read your partner's writing carefully. For each sentence, circle the choice that best describes the writing. Respond to the prompts.

1. The main idea is clear.
   Needs improvement   Satisfactory   Excellent

2. The details support the main idea.
   Needs improvement   Satisfactory   Excellent

3. The ideas flow smoothly and in an orderly way.
   Needs improvement   Satisfactory   Excellent

4. The structure clearly follows the Hamburger Model (introduction, body, conclusion).
   Needs improvement   Satisfactory   Excellent

5. The vocabulary is rich and varied.
   Needs improvement   Satisfactory   Excellent

The writing is strong in these ways:

____

____

____

The writing could be improved in these ways:

____

____

____

Name: ______________________ Date: __________

Activity 18C

Self-Review of Unit Research Project

Directions: For each sentence, circle the choice that best describes your unit research project at this point. Respond to the prompts.

1. The issue or problem is clearly defined.
   Needs improvement   Satisfactory   Excellent
2. The sources are diverse.
   Needs improvement   Satisfactory   Excellent
3. Key sources are summarized.
   Needs improvement   Satisfactory   Excellent
4. Interview or survey questions are included.
   Needs improvement   Satisfactory   Excellent
5. Results from interviews and/or surveys are summarized.
   Needs improvement   Satisfactory   Excellent
6. Results are reported appropriately.
   Needs improvement   Satisfactory   Excellent
7. The data are interpreted appropriately.
   Needs improvement   Satisfactory   Excellent
8. Implications are drawn from the data.
   Needs improvement   Satisfactory   Excellent
9. Reasonable conclusions are stated.
   Needs improvement   Satisfactory   Excellent
10. The paper is free of mechanical errors.
   Needs improvement   Satisfactory   Excellent

My project is strong in these ways:

____

____

____

My project could be improved in these ways:

____

____

____

Walking

Linda Hogan

It began in dark and underground weather, a slow hunger moving toward light. It grew in a dry gully beside the road where I live, a place where entire hillsides are sometimes yellow, windblown tides of sunflower plants. But this one was different. It was alone, and larger than the countless others who had established their lives further up the hill. This one was a traveler, a settler, and like a dream beginning in conflict, it grew where the land had been disturbed.

I saw it first in early summer. It was a green and sleeping bud, raising itself toward the sun. Ants worked around the unopened bloom, gathering aphids and sap. A few days later, it was a tender young flower, soft and new, with a pale green center and a troop of silver gray insects climbing up and down the stalk.

Over the summer this sunflower grew into a plant of incredible beauty, turning its face daily toward the sun in the most subtle of ways, the black center of it dark and alive with a deep blue light, as if flint had sparked an elemental fire there, in community with rain, mineral, mountain air, and sand.

As summer changed from green to yellow there were new visitors daily: the lace-winged insects, the bees whose legs were fat with pollen, and grasshoppers with their clattering wings and desperate hunger. There were other lives I missed, lives too small or hidden to see. It was as if this plant with its host of lives was a society, one in which moment by moment, depending on light and moisture, there was great and diverse change.

There were changes in the next larger world around the plant as well. One day I rounded a bend in the road to find the disturbing sight of a dead horse, black and still against a hillside, eyes rolled back. Another day I was nearly lifted by a wind and sandstorm so fierce and hot that I had to wait for it to pass before I could return home. On this day the faded dry petals of the sunflower were swept across the land. That was when the birds arrived to carry the new seeds to another future.

In this one plant, in one summer season, a drama of need and survival took place. Hungers were filled. Insects coupled. There was escape, exhaustion, and death. Lives touched down a moment and were gone.

I was an outsider. I only watched. I never learned the sunflower's golden language or the tongues of its citizens. I had a small understanding, nothing more than a shallow observation of the flower, insects, and birds. But they knew what to do, how to live. An old voice from somewhere, gene or cell, told the plant how to evade the pull of gravity and find its way upward, how to open. It was instinct, intuition, necessity. A certain knowing directed the seed-bearing birds on paths to ancestral homelands they had never seen. They believed it. They followed.

There are other summons and calls, some even more mysterious than those commandments to birds or those survival journeys of insects. In bamboo plants, for instance, with their thin green canopy of light and golden stalks that creak in the wind. Once a century, all of a certain kind of bamboo flower on the same day. Whether they are in Malaysia or in a greenhouse in Minnesota makes no difference, nor does the age or size of the plant. They flower. Some current of an inner language passes between them, through space and separation, in ways we cannot explain in our language. They are all, somehow, one plant, each with a share of communal knowledge.

John Hay, in *The Immortal Wilderness,* has written: "There are occasions when you can hear the mysterious language of the Earth, in water, or coming through the trees, emanating from the mosses, seeping through the undercurrents of the soil, but you have to be willing to wait and receive."

Sometimes I hear it talking. The light of the sunflower was one language, but there are others, more audible. Once, in the redwood forest, I heard a beat, something like a drum or heart coming from the ground and trees and wind. That underground current stirred a kind of knowing inside me, a kinship and longing, a dream barely remembered that disappeared back to the body.

Another time, there was the booming voice of an ocean storm thundering from far out at sea, telling about what lived in the distance, about the rough water that would arrive, wave after wave revealing the disturbance at the center.

Tonight I walk. I am watching the sky. I think of the people who came before me and how they knew the placement of stars in the sky, watched the moving sun long and hard enough to witness how a certain angle of light touched a stone only once a year. Without written records, they knew the gods of every night, the small, fine details of the world around them and of immensity above them.

Walking, I can almost hear the redwoods beating. And the oceans are above me here, rolling clouds, heavy and dark, considering snow. On the dry, red road, I pass the place of the sunflower, that dark and secret location where creation took place. I wonder if it will return this summer, if it will multiply and move up to the other stand of flowers in a territorial struggle.

It's winter and there is smoke from the fires. The square, lighted windows of houses are fogging over. It is a world of elemental attention, of all things working together, listening to what speaks in the blood. Whichever road I follow, I walk in the land of many gods, and they love and eat one another.

Walking, I am listening to a deeper way. Suddenly all my ancestors are behind me. Be still, they say. Watch and listen. You are the result of the love of thousands.

Name: ______________________________ Date: ________________

Activity 19A

Literature Web

Directions: Complete the Literature Web for "Walking."

Key Words

Feelings

Ideas

Title

Images/Symbols

Structure

Name: ________________________________ Date: ______________

Activity 19B

Vocabulary Web

Directions: Complete the Vocabulary Web for one of the following words: *aphids, elemental, intuition, communal,* or *audible.*

Word Families

Synonyms

Antonyms

Dictionary Definition

Word

Sentence in Text

Analysis

Part of Speech

Origin

Stems

Student Example

Name: ______________________________ Date: ______________

Literature Web

Directions: Complete the Literature Web for *My Daniel.*

Key Words

____

____

____

____

____

____

Feelings

____

____

____

____

____

____

Ideas

____

____

____

____

____

____

____

____

Title

____

____

____

____

Images/Symbols

____

____

____

____

____

____

____

____

Structure

____

____

____

____

Name: ______________________________ Date: ______________

Activity 20B

Hamburger Model: Titles, Good and Bad

Directions: Use the Hamburger Model to organize your ideas for a persuasive paragraph either defending the title of one of the two novels you read or arguing for a new title. Refer to your Literature Webs and Literature Journal entries for the novel as needed.

Introduction (State your opinion.)

____

____

Elaboration	**Elaboration**	**Elaboration**
______________	______________	______________
______________	______________	______________
Reason	**Reason**	**Reason**
______________	______________	______________
______________	______________	______________
Elaboration	**Elaboration**	**Elaboration**
______________	______________	______________
______________	______________	______________

Conclusion

____

____

Name: ______________________ Date: ______________

Literature Web

Directions: Complete the Literature Web for Sonnet II.

Key Words

Feelings

Ideas

Title

Images/Symbols

Structure

Sonnet II

William Shakespeare

When forty winters shall besiege thy brow
And dig deep trenches in thy beauty's field,
Thy youth's proud livery, so gazed on now,
Will be a tatter'd weed, of small worth held:
Then being ask'd where all thy beauty lies,
Where all the treasure of thy lusty days,
To say, within thine own deep-sunken eyes,
Were an all-eating shame and thriftless praise.
How much more praise deserved thy beauty's use,
If thou couldst answer "This fair child of mine
Shall sum my count and make my old excuse,"
Proving his beauty by succession thine!
This were to be new made when thou art old,
And see thy blood warm when thou feel'st it cold.

Name: ______________________________ Date: ______________

Activity 21A The Shakespearean Sonnet

The sonnet is a lyric poem of 14 lines that was first developed in 13th-century Italy. Though sonnets may be written with many different rhyme schemes, William Shakespeare used the same form for all 154 of his sonnets.

The Shakespearean sonnet can be divided into three stanzas of four lines each, with an ending couplet.

Define *couplet.* ______________________________

Within each stanza, every other line rhymes. The two lines of the couplet rhyme with each other. This rhyme scheme can be written as ABAB/CDCD/EFEF/GG.

Which pairs of words rhyme in the second stanza? ______________

____

The lines are written in iambic pentameter. This metric pattern consists of ten syllables, with every second syllable stressed: da-DUM, da-DUM, da-DUM, da-DUM, da-DUM. Note, however, that a good poet varies the rhythm somewhat to emphasize certain words.

Underline the stressed syllables in the first line of the sonnet:
When forty winters shall besiege thy brow.

Like many sonnets, most of Shakespeare's sonnets present an argument. The first stanza poses a problem. The second stanza complicates the problem. The third stanza proposes a solution. The couplet wraps up or extends the argument.

What is the argument in Sonnet II? ______________________________

____

____

Name: ______________________________ Date: ________________

Activity 21B

Vocabulary Web

Directions: Complete the Vocabulary Web for one of the following words: *besiege, thriftless,* or *succession.*

Word Families

Synonyms

Antonyms

Dictionary Definition

Word

Sentence in Text

Analysis

Part of Speech

Origin

Stems

Student Example

Name: ______________________________ Date: ______________

Oral Presentation Evaluation Form

Speaker: ______________ **Assignment:** ____________________

Directions: For 1–8, circle the choice that describes the presentation. Then complete the two sentences.

Content and Organization

1. The purpose of the presentation was clear.
   Needs improvement Satisfactory Excellent

2. The speaker included details that supported the main idea.
   Needs improvement Satisfactory Excellent

3. The speaker addressed opposing points of view.
   Needs improvement Satisfactory Excellent

4. The speaker showed knowledge of the subject.
   Needs improvement Satisfactory Excellent

5. The speaker closed the presentation with a strong, interesting idea that restated the purpose.
   Needs improvement Satisfactory Excellent

Delivery

6. The speaker made good eye contact with the audience.
   Needs improvement Satisfactory Excellent

7. The speaker spoke loudly enough for the entire audience to hear.
   Needs improvement Satisfactory Excellent

8. The speaker's words were clear and could be understood.
   Needs improvement Satisfactory Excellent

The best part of this presentation was:

____

____

____

____

A suggestion for improvement is:

____

____

____

____

Name: ______________________________ Date: ______________

Evaluation Form: Standards of Reasoning

Directions: For 1–7, circle the choice that best describes the argument in the presentation. Then complete the sentence.

Speaker: ______________ **Assignment:** ____________________

1. Enough reasons were given to make the argument convincing.
   Needs improvement Satisfactory Excellent

2. The supporting evidence was factual and correct.
   Needs improvement Satisfactory Excellent

3. The reasons were clear and explained thoroughly.
   Needs improvement Satisfactory Excellent

4. The reasons and evidence were specific.
   Needs improvement Satisfactory Excellent

5. The reasons were strong and important.
   Needs improvement Satisfactory Excellent

6. The argument was logical, presented in sentences that seemed to go together in a sequence that made sense.
   Needs improvement Satisfactory Excellent

7. The explanation of the issue was fair.
   Needs improvement Satisfactory Excellent

The strongest part of the argument was:

____

____

____

____

Name: ______________________________ Date: ______________

Activity 22C Research Project Assessment

Directions: For 1–10, circle the choice that best describes each aspect of the project. Then complete the two sentences.

1. The issue or problem is clearly defined.
   Needs improvement Satisfactory Excellent

2. The sources are diverse.
   Needs improvement Satisfactory Excellent

3. Key sources are summarized.
   Needs improvement Satisfactory Excellent

4. Interview or survey questions are included.
   Needs improvement Satisfactory Excellent

5. Results from interviews and/or surveys are summarized.
   Needs improvement Satisfactory Excellent

6. Results are reported appropriately.
   Needs improvement Satisfactory Excellent

7. The data are interpreted appropriately.
   Needs improvement Satisfactory Excellent

8. Implications are drawn from the data.
   Needs improvement Satisfactory Excellent

9. Reasonable conclusions are stated.
   Needs improvement Satisfactory Excellent

10. The paper is free of mechanical errors.
    Needs improvement Satisfactory Excellent

The strengths of the research project are:

____

____

____

____

The areas needing improvement are:

____

____

____

____

Name: ________________________________ Date: ________________

Final Writing Assignment

Directions: A character in the novel *O Pioneers!* by Willa Cather states, "There are only two or three human stories, and they go on repeating themselves as fiercely as if they had never happened before." Think about how this statement relates to the unit readings and to cyclic patterns of change. Do you agree or disagree with the statement? Write a persuasive essay explaining whether or not you agree and why. Use varied and specific examples from the readings and your own experience to support your reasons. Use the Hamburger Model on Activity 23B to help you organize your ideas.

Name: ______________________ Date: ____________

Activity 23B

Hamburger Model: Final Writing Assignment

Directions: Use the Hamburger Model to plan your response to the assignment on Activity 23A. Draft your response on a separate sheet of paper.

Introduction
(State your opinion.)

____

____

Elaboration	**Elaboration**	**Elaboration**
____	____	____
____	____	____
____	____	____
Reason	**Reason**	**Reason**
____	____	____
____	____	____
____	____	____
Elaboration	**Elaboration**	**Elaboration**
____	____	____
____	____	____
____	____	____

Conclusion

____

____

From "Little Gidding"

T. S. Eliot

What we call the beginning is often the end
And to make an end is to make a beginning.
The end is where we start from. And every phrase ...
Every phrase and every sentence is an end and a beginning,
Every poem an epitaph. ...
... A people without history
Is not redeemed from time, for history is a pattern
Of timeless moments. So, while the light fails
On a winter's afternoon, in a secluded chapel
History is now and England.

With the drawing of this Love and the voice of this Calling

We shall not cease from exploration
And the end of all our exploring
Will be to arrive where we started
And know the place for the first time. ...

Name: ______________________________ Date: ________________

Activity 24A Writing Portfolio Assessment

Directions: Review your writing portfolio and respond to the following questions.

1. What do you think is the biggest change in your writing from the first piece to the last?

____

____

2. How has the organization of your writing improved? Give examples of this change.

____

____

3. How have the ideas in your writing improved? Give examples of this change.

____

____

4. What do you think is the best aspect of your writing right now?

____

____

5. What aspects of your writing would you like to improve?

____

____

Inspecting Our Own Ideas: Student Grammar Study

By Michael C. Thompson

As you begin to read this short study of grammar and to think about the ideas you will find here, you should know that there is one important purpose for what you are doing. It is not to learn a large number of facts, or to memorize terms, or to score points. Lots of grammar books can help you learn facts and terms. This study is different. Its purpose is to show you the deeper meaning of grammar that is usually missing from the grammar fact books—the part that many people never understand.

What is this deeper meaning?

It is that grammar is a kind of magic lens, a secret thinking method we can use to peek inside our own minds and to detect the designs of our own ideas.

Using grammar this way, we can learn about ourselves, learn about what makes us human, learn about why some ideas are clear and others are confused, learn about beautiful ways to share our thoughts with other people.

In order to make the most of what you will read, you should understand from the beginning that, even though there will be facts and details to learn, the facts are not the point. The point is the point. And so as you read, do what the coaches always tell you: keep your eye on the ball.

Do not forget that you are concentrating on the deep thinking, the deep meaning, the ability to appreciate the real power of grammar.

The best way to do this is to begin by previewing the study with your teacher. Look over it together, and agree on how much you should read in your first session. Then go read, and think, and reread. Make notes on your ideas and on the questions you have that the reading doesn't answer. Then meet with your teacher to talk about what you have learned and to look over any of the written exercises you may have done. Keep working in this way until you have read the entire grammar study and can discuss it completely with your teacher or other students, depending upon your class situation.

Remember that grammar is a kind of higher order thinking, like logic or mathematics. Grammar can show us secrets that no other thinking method can show us. If you read and think carefully, you will never forget that grammar is a wonderful tool for the mind.

1. Ideas, Language, and Grammar

How do we talk to each other?

How do we write to each other?

How do we read what someone else has written?

We use **language**. Language is our way of putting words together to make our **ideas**.

Any time we use words to say *something about something*, that is an idea!

We have to say *something . . . about something.*

In other words, an idea is made of *two parts*. One part is *what we are talking about*, and the other part is *what we are saying about it.*

We might say something about ourselves. Or we might say something about an object, such as a distant spiral galaxy in deep space, or a glowing hologram, or a thundering Triceratops. We might say something about wispy, white, cirrostratus clouds in a blue, summer sky. If we did that, we might say: "Wispy, white, cirrostratus clouds in a blue, summer sky floated high over my head."

Do you see the two parts of that idea?

What we are talking about:

Wispy, white, cirrostratus clouds in a blue, summer sky

What we are saying about it:

floated high over my head.

In this idea, we are using words in language to make an idea about cirrostratus clouds.

Of course, if wispy, white clouds in a blue, summer sky floated high over our heads, there would probably be a bird—high, high up—flying near the cloud. This would be a strong bird indeed, since cirrostratus clouds are found at 20,000 feet and higher! There would probably be summer insects buzzing around, eating fresh leaves and drinking nectar from the flowers. The grass would probably be cool and feel good on our bare feet. It would be nice.

Let's get back to language and ideas. Another idea could be, "I'm nobody." In this idea, we are saying something about something. Part one: we are talking about ourselves. Part two: what are we saying about ourselves? That we are nobody. Of course, this idea comes from a very famous poem by Emily Dickinson, one of America's very greatest poets. And when she said "I'm nobody," she was using irony to change the meaning from bad to good! If you read the rest of the poem, you will see how quickly Emily Dickinson accomplishes this change of meaning.

So, ideas have two parts.

Guess what? We have a very special way to study ideas that we make out of words in language. This special way to study language is called grammar.

Grammar Is a Way of Thinking about Language.

Using grammar, we can inspect one of our own language ideas, and see how language is made! We can do lots of things with grammar. We can find an idea's two parts, and we can find all of the groups of words in the idea, and we can even look at each word by itself and see what it does to make the idea work. This helps us to understand ourselves, and to understand how we think! In the pages that follow, you will learn about grammar, and about how grammar helps us to understand our own ideas.

Review

Let's look again at the ideas we have discussed. Think carefully about each of these points:

Language: Our way of putting words together to express our ideas.

Idea: A two-part thought about something.

The two parts of an idea: What we are talking about, and what we are saying about it.

Grammar: A special way of thinking about language.

2. Sentence: A Subject and Its Predicate

In grammar, we have a special word to describe an idea that is made of two parts. This special word is **sentence**. A sentence is an idea. We sometimes say that a sentence is a **complete thought**, but this is just a different way of saying the same thing—that a sentence is an idea.

Would you like to know an interesting fact? Our English word *sentence* comes from a very old word, *sententia*, which was a word used thousands of years ago in an ancient language called *Latin*. Latin was the language spoken by the ancient Romans of Italy. To the ancient Romans, the word *sententia* meant "way of thinking." Latin was also the source of our English word *cirrostratus*, which we saw in the first section of this discussion. The word *cirrostratus* comes from the Latin stems *cirrus*, meaning "curl," and *stratus*, meaning "layer." Cirrostratus clouds form a thin, "curly layer" of clouds. We will see that many of the words used in grammar have very logical meanings that are based on ancient Latin or Greek words.

Now, we learned that a sentence is an idea that is complete. But what makes a sentence's idea complete?

It is complete because it has both of the two parts that it needs to make sense to someone. Until it has both of these two important parts, it is not finished, not complete.

Let's think about this for a minute. If I wish to understand you, then there are two things that I need to know:

1. I need to know what you are *talking about*, and
2. I need to know *what you are saying about it.*

If I do know these two things, then I can understand you. If, however, I do not know what you are talking about, or if I do not know what you are saying about it, then I will not understand you.

Grammar gives us names for these two parts of the sentence. The first part of the sentence, what it is about, is called the **complete subject**. The second part of the sentence, what we are saying about the subject, is called the **complete predicate**. Let's look at some examples:

Complete Subject (What the idea is about)	**Complete Predicate** (What we are saying about the subject)
The crane	fishes patiently in the lake.
They	would banish us.
The people	could fly.
Crick and Watson	discovered DNA.
I	loved my friend.
Lenny	is a boy in my class.
That day	was one of the coldest.
He	had several beds of zinnias.
She	had a little thin face.
I	am

Notice that a sentence does not have to be long. Sometimes a sentence only has two words in it. "Pterodactyls landed" is a sentence. Even though it is short, it has a subject, *Pterodactyls*, and a predicate, *landed.*

Do you know what pterodactyls were? They were flying dinosaurs that had wings of skin, and that became extinct at the end of the Mesozoic era. In Arizona fossil pterodactyls have been found that had 40-foot wingspans. They are called *pterodactyls* because they had clawed fingers in the middle of their wings, and so their scientific name comes from the ancient Greek *pter,* which means wing, and *dactyl,* which means finger. A second question: Do you know what the Mesozoic era was? Well, *meso* means middle, and *zo* means animal. The Mesozoic era was a geologic era in the earth's history that occurred after the Paleozoic era and before the Cenozoic era, from 230,000,000 years ago until 65,000,000 years ago. The Mesozoic era featured the rise and fall of the dinosaurs and the appearance of birds, grasses, and flowering plants. If you are really adventurous, you will go look up the Paleozoic era, and see what happened then!

Now, let's make some new sentences! I will give you a subject or predicate to start with, and then you can think of your own way to finish the sentence. Sometimes I will give you a subject and leave the predicate blank, and sometimes I will give you a predicate and leave the subject blank. Fill in the blanks with subjects or predicates that help the sentence make sense. For example, if I give you a subject, such as "The star cruiser," you could fill in the predicate blank with a predicate that you imagine. You might complete the sentence by writing, "rumbled toward the icy planet." (Of course, nothing *rumbles* in space, since sound does not carry in a vacuum.)

New Sentences

Complete Subject (What the idea is about)	Complete Predicate (What we are saying about the subject)
1. F. L. Wright, the famous architect,	________________
2. Egyptian hieroglyphics	________________
3. The red laser beam	________________
4. ________________	shone across the Mediterranean.
5. ________________	quietly munched the bamboo shoots.
6. ________________	climbed aboard the Hispaniola.
7. The people of ancient Carthage	________________
8. Beethoven's best symphony	________________
9. ________________	is my favorite work of art.
10. ________________	littered the laboratory.

Notice that until you completed the subject or predicate, none of your sentences made sense. A subject or a predicate by itself is not an idea; it is only a fragment, or piece of an idea. A sentence fragment is a piece of a sentence that only makes an incomplete thought. A sentence fragment needs to be finished, just like the subjects and predicates above needed to be finished.

How would I have finished the ten sentences you just worked on? Well, I might have finished them this way:

Complete Subject (What the idea is about)	Complete Predicate (What we are saying about the subject)
1. F. L. Wright, the famous architect,	*designed houses to match the landscape.*
2. Egyptian hieroglyphics	*are made of little pictures.*
3. The red laser beam	*could be seen from the moon.*
4. *The ship's festive lights*	shone across the Mediterranean.
5. *The panda bear*	quietly munched the bamboo shoots.
6. *The wide-eyed, young boy*	climbed aboard the Hispaniola.

7. The people of ancient Carthage *waved good-bye to Hannibal.*
8. Beethoven's best symphony *is a musical masterpiece.*
9. *Van Gogh's self-portrait* is my favorite work of art.
10. *Empty pizza boxes* littered the laboratory.

By the way, the *Hispaniola* was the sailing ship in Robert Louis Stevenson's wonderful classic, *Treasure Island*, which is about young Jim Hawkins and his adventures with the dastardly pirates led by Long John Silver. If you have not read this masterpiece, you are in for a great time. I know you would enjoy looking up the famous architect, Frank Lloyd Wright (find photographs of his buildings), as well as the ancient general Hannibal, the great composer Ludwig van Beethoven (listen to a recording of his famous Fifth Symphony), and the Dutch painter Vincent Van Gogh (look at a reproduction of his painting *Starry Night*).

Now you can make up some sentences of your own. Write the subjects in the blanks at the left, and write the predicates in the blanks at the right. Use your creativity and imagination to write some unexpected and interesting sentences.

Sentences

Complete Subject (What the idea is **about**)	**Complete Predicate** (What **we are saying** about the subject)
1. ______________________	1. ______________________
2. ______________________	2. ______________________
3. ______________________	3. ______________________

Review

Now let's look again at the new ideas we have learned about language and sentences.

Our way of putting words together to make our ideas is called **language**.

A two-part thought about something is called an **idea**.

What we are talking about and what we are saying about it are the **two parts of an idea**.

A special way of thinking about language is called **grammar**.

In grammar, we call a two-part idea a **sentence**.

The two parts of the sentence are called the **subject** and the **predicate**.

What the sentence is about is called the **subject**.

What we are saying about the subject is called the **predicate**.

A piece of a sentence that is not complete is only a **fragment**.

What Is a Sentence Like?

Now that you understand that a sentence is made of two parts—a subject the sentence is about and a predicate that says something about the subject—think of some other things that also have two parts. For example, an egg has both a white and a yolk inside. A basketball goal has a backboard and a rim. A bicycle wheel has a center and a rim. A person has a first name and a last name. Make a list of things that, like sentences, have two parts. After my first examples, fill in your own.

The Thing	Part One	Part Two
egg	white	yolk
mouth	upper lip	lower lip
shooting an arrow	pull back	let go
echo	sound goes away	sound comes back
______________	______________	______________
______________	______________	______________
______________	______________	______________
______________	______________	______________
______________	______________	______________
______________	______________	______________
______________	______________	______________
______________	______________	______________

Now that you have a list of things that have two parts, which one of these things in your list do you think is really most like a sentence, with its two subject/predicate parts? What is the best comparison? Think about it carefully, and then explain your choice:

Did you enjoy thinking that way? Thinking up comparisons between two different things is a special and important kind of thinking, called *synthesis*. Synthesis is the ability to see connections, or similarities, or relationships between things that seem unconnected at first. When we use synthesis to see hidden connections, we are often surprised to learn how similar things are, and how much everything is connected.

A vocabulary note: The word *subject* contains two ancient Latin word pieces, or stems, that we see in many words, *sub* and *ject*. The stem *sub* means "under," and we see *sub* in words such as *submarine* and *submerge*. The stem *ject* means "throw," and we see *ject* in words such as *eject* and *dejected*. So the word *subject* actually contains a picture: the *subject* of a sentence is the part that is "thrown down" for discussion. Look up some of the following example words in your dictionary, and see if you can understand why they mean what they mean:

Stem	**Meaning**	**Example Words**
sub	under	submarine, submerge, subdue, subtract, subside, subordinate
ject	throw	reject, dejected, interject, eject, conjecture, project, adjective, object

3. Clauses: The Sentences Within Sentences

There is another surprising fact about the way we make our ideas into sentences. Many of the sentences that we use are just like the ones we have already studied. They have a subject, and then a predicate, and then the sentence ends. Sometimes, however, our ideas get so connected that we like to join simple ideas together into a longer, more complicated idea. In other words, sometimes, we join little related sentences together into a big sentence. For example, we might have these two sentences:

Congress passed the bill. The president signed it into law.

Each of these sentences has its own subject and predicate. But since these two sentences describe something that happened in a connected event, we can connect the sentences together into a longer sentence:

Congress passed the bill, and the president signed it into law.

Now the two little sentences make one long sentence, and it has one subject and predicate, followed by a second subject and predicate, all in one sentence!

Congress	passed the bill,	and	the president	signed it into law.
subject	predicate		subject	predicate

When we join little sentences this way into a longer sentence of subject/predicate chains, we call each little subject/predicate group a clause.

Congress passed the bill,	and	the president signed it into law.
first clause		second clause

When there is only one subject/predicate set in the sentence, we say that the sentence has one **clause.**

Our word clause comes from the ancient Latin word *claudere*, which meant "to close" to the Romans. This makes sense even now because a clause is a group of words in which an idea gets opened, and closed! The idea is opened when we introduce a subject, and then it is closed when we provide the predicate. In a long sentence made of many clauses, we open and close a number of related ideas in a row. Let's look at some examples of clauses in sentences. Notice that each clause has its own subject and its own predicate:

Clauses in Sentences

1. Our forefathers brought forth upon this continent a new nation.

subject — predicate

a one-clause sentence

2. I will arise, and I will go now.

subj. predicate — subj. predicate

first clause — second clause

a two-clause sentence

3. Robert Frost has miles to go before he sleeps.

subject — predicate — subj. predicate

first clause — second clause

a two-clause sentence

4. When the attack finally begins, you sneak up quietly, and

subject — predicate — subj. — predicate

first clause — second clause

the gang throws balloons.

subject — predicate

third clause

a three-clause sentence

See? We can make long sentences out of any number of related ideas!

But why is it important to know this?

By using grammar to inspect our own ideas, we have discovered that our wonderful brains can understand ideas and the relationships between different ideas so well and so quickly that we can connect these ideas into sentences of clauses faster than we can even speak. We can do it without even knowing we are doing it, and before we even have a name for it. It is only now, when we use grammar to inspect our ideas, that we begin to realize what powerful things our minds are. The grammar of clauses shows us how our minds build beautiful structures of ideas.

4. Parts of Speech: The Kinds of Words

One thing you have noticed about all ideas or sentences: every sentence is made of words. A word is a group of sounds or letters that means something. In the sentence, "The famous author Robert Louis Stevenson (1850–1894) wrote the novel, Treasure Island," there are 11 words. For example, Robert is a word and the is a word. We always put blank spaces between words in a written sentence. If you look at a college dictionary, you will see that we have many thousands of words in our language. In fact, there are far more words than anyone could ever learn!

Just imagine that you traveled to a land far, far away.

(One faraway land is Nepal, near Tibet in the continent of Asia, where Mount Everest, the highest mountain in the world, is. Mount Everest is 29,028 feet high, and it is in the Himalayan mountain range. It is so high that it has only been climbed a few times. Nepal's high-altitude capital is Katmandu. There is a wonderful novel you will want to read one day, *Lost Horizon*, written by James Hilton in 1933, that depicts Nepal under the fictitious name of "Shangri-La.")

Now, just imagine that you travel to a land far, far away, and the gray-bearded king of the land says, "You may have all of the treasures in my kingdom if you can tell me how many kinds of words there are." The king then looks down to the green valleys far, far below, and an icy wind comes down from the frozen peaks above, and blows through your hair.

What would you say? There are thousands and thousands of words in the dictionary. Are there thousands of kinds of words? Are there hundreds of kinds of words?

Well, you are in luck, because if you set off on an adventure one day, you will be prepared with the knowledge that there are only eight kinds of words! Just imagine! All of those words in the dictionary can be put into only eight piles, and the eight different kinds of words are easy to learn. We call the eight kinds of words the eight **parts of speech** because all of our speech can be *parted* into only eight piles of words.

The names of the eight parts of speech are the *noun, pronoun, adjective, verb, adverb, preposition, conjunction,* and *interjection.* In a sentence, each part of speech has something different to do. And since a sentence might only have two words in it, you can tell that not every sentence uses all eight parts of speech.

The only parts of speech that have to be in a sentence are the noun or pronoun and the verb. Can you guess why? Let's learn about the eight parts of speech and their functions (uses). As you read the following pages, study the definitions, examples, and discussions of the eight parts of speech carefully and slowly.

The Parts of Speech

Part of Speech	**Function**	**Examples**
noun (n.)	**name of something**	***Mary, dog, garden, sound***

A noun is the name of a person, *Picasso*, or the name of a place, *Amsterdam*, or the name of a thing, *aurora*. The sentence "The wind in the willows whispered in the leaves" has three nouns: wind, willows, and leaves. Nouns give us names for things!

Proper nouns are the names of specific people, places, or things. Otherwise, they are common nouns. Study the following examples to see the difference.

Proper Nouns	*Common Nouns*
John	boy
Chicago	city
Statue of Liberty	monument

Nouns can be **singular**, like *dog*, or **plural**, like *dogs*. Proper nouns, like *Istanbul*, are capitalized, but common nouns, like *boy*, are not capitalized.

Part of Speech	**Function**	**Examples**
pronoun (pron.)	**replaces a noun**	***I, she, him, it, them***

A pronoun is a short word that replaces a usually longer noun so that we can speak faster. For example, instead of always saying a person's name, such as *Abraham Lincoln*, in a sentence, we can say *he*. In the sentence "He was born in a log cabin in Illinois," the words *Abraham Lincoln* have been replaced by the short pronoun *he*. Pronouns make language fast!

Two common kinds of pronouns are the **subject pronouns**:

I, you, he, she, it, we, you, they

and the **object pronouns**:

me, you, him, her, it, us, you, them

We have learned that every sentence has a subject and a predicate. Also, every subject contains either a noun or a pronoun. This noun or pronoun that the sentence is about is sometimes called the **simple subject**. The **complete subject** is the simple subject and all the words around it that modify it. Consider the following example:

The big, brown bear lumbered into the woods.

The word *bear* is the simple subject. *The big, brown bear* is the complete subject.

adjective (adj.)	**modifies a noun or pronoun**	***red, tall, fast, good, the***

To modify is to *change*. An adjective is a word that changes the meaning of a noun or pronoun. For example, for the noun *tree*, we can change it by saying *tall* tree, or *Christmas* tree, or *cherry* tree, and each of these different adjectives changes (we sometimes say *modifies*) the noun and gives us a different picture in our minds. Another example: the noun *garden* could be modified by either the adjective *flower* or the adjective *secret*. We could talk about a *flower* garden, but we could use a different adjective and talk about a *secret* garden instead, and that would modify the idea. Some adjectives are the opposites of one another: a *fast* car is the opposite of a *slow* car.

The most common adjectives are the three little words *a, an,* and *the*. These three adjectives are called the articles. The word *the* is called the **definite article**, and the words *a* and *an* are called the **indefinite articles**.

Notice that the noun, pronoun, and adjective go together and work together. The nouns name things, the pronouns replace the nouns, and the adjectives modify either nouns or pronouns. You could say that the noun, with its supporting pronouns and adjectives, forms a little noun system, like the sun with its planets.

verb (v.)	**an action or equals word**	***jumps, fell, is***

Every sentence contains a verb, which is sometimes called the **simple predicate**. The **complete predicate** is the simple predicate and all the words around it that modify it. For example:

> The big, brown bear lumbered into the woods.

The word *lumbered* is the simple predicate. *Lumbered into the woods* is the complete predicate.

There are two kinds of verbs.

Action verbs show action: they show people and things doing things. Look at the action verbs in these sentences: the dog *barked*. The tall man *grinned*. My best friend *reads* lots of books. We *drove* to Florida. Mary *opened* her brown eyes.

Linking verbs are equals words. They show that two things are the same. For example, in the sentence "Siegfried is a good student." the verb *is* means that Siegfried and the good student are the same person. Siegfried IS the good student.

Action: Michelangelo ran after the ball.

Linking: Michelangelo is good at soccer.

Action: Donatello drew a sketch.

Linking: Donatello is a genius.

Action: Raphael plays baseball in the spring.

Linking: Raphael is a pitcher on the baseball team.

My favorite linking verb sentence is by the poet Marianne Moore, who said that poems *are* imaginary gardens with real toads in them. Don't you like that idea?

Parts of the sentence: We have learned about two parts of the sentence already, the **simple subject** and the **simple predicate** or verb. Well, there are two other parts of the sentence you can identify if you know what kind of verb you have. When an action verb sentence shows the subject doing something to something, as in the sentence "The dog bit the mailman," we call the noun or pronoun that receives the action a **direct object**. When a linking verb sentence shows that the subject is *equal to* something else, as in the sentence "The dog is a poodle," we call the noun or pronoun that is linked to the subject a **subject complement**.

Direct object: Achilles grabbed the *warrior.*

Subject complement: Achilles was a *warrior.*

Notice that the only way to tell whether the second noun in these sentences is a direct object or a subject complement is to look at the verb. If a sentence contains an action verb, it might have a direct object, but if the sentence contains a linking verb, it might have a subject complement. This is a very advanced grammar idea, and it gives us deep insight into the way we form our own ideas.

Tense: Another very important fact: verbs change, according to the *time* they are describing. The time of the verb is called the verb **tense**. The three most familiar verb tenses are the **present tense**, the **past tense**, and the **future tense**. The verb to *believe*, for example, takes these forms:

Present tense: I *believe* in miracles.

Past tense: I *believed* in miracles.

Future tense: I *will believe* in miracles.

adverb (adv.)	**modifies a verb, adj., or adv.**	***quickly, slowly, well***

An adverb is a word that modifies or changes the meaning of a verb, an adjective, or another adverb.

Adverb modifies verb: I swam *quickly*.

Adverb modifies adverb: I swam *very* quickly.

Adverb modifies adjective: I saw a *very* red star.

Before you continue reading, study these three examples very carefully, and make sure you understand every part of speech in every sentence.

Notice that many adverbs end in *ly*, such as *quickly, slowly, loudly, nearly, badly,* and *hungrily*.

Notice that the verb and adverb form a little system together. Just as the noun is often accompanied by an adjective, the verb is often accompanied by an adverb that gives it new meaning.

Just as adjectives help us adjust the meanings of nouns when the nouns are not quite what we mean, adverbs help us adjust the meanings of verbs. Adjectives and adverbs are modifiers that help us adjust the meanings of nouns and verbs.

preposition (prep.) **shows relationship** ***in, on, beside, after***

A **preposition** is a word that shows how two things are *related* to each other in space or time. Space examples: The dog was *on* the dock. The book is *in* the drawer. The boy was *inside* the secret garden. The garden was *behind* the wall. Time examples: The movie is *after* the news. My birthday is *before* yours. She got sick *during* the game. Prepositions are little words, but they are very important because they show where everything is in space and time. Prepositions let us make ideas that show how the world is arranged!

Another interesting fact about prepositions is that they are always found in little word groups, such as *in* the box, *on* the dock, *under* the bed, *around* the world, and *over* the rainbow. These little word groups always begin with prepositions, and they are called **prepositional phrases**.

In fact, the word *preposition* is made of the Latin *pre*, which means *before*, and the word *position*. A preposition is called a preposition because its *position is always before* the other words in the prepositional phrase! It has the preposition.

conjunction (conj.) **joins words** ***and, or, but, so, yet***

A conjunction is a word that joins two other words together into a pair. Michael *and* David ate many hot dogs. By using the conjunction *and*, we can join the two nouns *Michael* and *David* together so we can talk about them both at once, as a pair. We can use a conjunction to join two pronouns: Give the lithograph to him *or* her. If we want to, we can even use a conjunction to join two verbs: Mary thought *and* wondered. We can use a conjunction to join two adverbs: He spoke quickly, *but* confidently. Or we can use a conjunction to join two adjectives: The wall was high *and* dark. Conjunctions let us join things into pairs!

Would you like one more very interesting example? You can even use a conjunction to join two groups of words together. For example, you can use a conjunction to join two prepositional phrases together: The albatross flew over the ship *and* around the mast.

interjection (interj.)	**shows emotion**	***Oh, wow, yes, no, well***

Interjections do not do anything special, such as join words, or modify words, or replace words. All they do is show emotion. If we say, "Wow, you look nice!" the word *wow* just shows happiness or excitement. The most common interjections are the words *yes* and *no*. Another very common interjection is the word *oh*: Oh, yes, I like interjections. Do you?

A Vocabulary Note

The word *preposition* contains two ancient Latin word pieces, or stems, *pre*, and *pos*. We see these stems in many words. The stem *pre* means "before," and we see *pre* in words such as *predict* and *prepare*. The stem *pos* means "put," and we see *pos* in words such as *position* and *depose*. So the word preposition contains a picture: the preposition is the part that is "put before" the other words in the phrase. The word *conjunction* also contains stems that appear in many other words: *con* and *junct*. The stem *con* means "together," and the stem *junct* means "join." In the words *adverb* and *adjective*, we see the stem *ad*, which means "to," and the word *pronoun* contains the stem *pro*, which means "for" or sometimes "forward." Look up some of the following example words in your dictionary, and see if you can understand why they mean what they mean:

Stem	Meaning	Example Words
pre	before	predict, prepare, preliminary, preschool, preface, premonition
pos	put	position, depose, interpose, suppose, deposit, repose
con	together	conjunction, contact, connect, contiguous, contract, converge
junct	join	juncture, disjunction, injunction, adjunct, conjunction
ad	to	adjective, adverb, adherent, adjacent, adapt, admit
pro	for/forward	pronoun, propel, prophet, proponent, prominent, promote

Now, you know that the stem *ject* means "throw." In the word *object*, however, we also see the stem *ob*, which means "toward" or "about." We see the stem *ob* in many words: *object, obstacle, obdurate, oblique, obloquy, objurgate,* and *obscure*, for example. Use your dictionary to look up the full etymology of the word *object* and see if you can understand why we call objects *objects*. Then answer this question: How are direct objects in sentences similar to objects on the ground?

Review

Let's look again at what the eight kinds of words do. Study the parts of speech until you have their functions memorized. Make sure that you can remember some examples of each one.

noun	name of something	Mike, dog, tree, sound
	The *boy* listened to the *music of Verdi.*	

pronoun	replaces a noun	I, she, him, it, them
	She and *I* saw *him* and *her* at the Museum of Modern Art.	
adjective	modifies a noun or pronoun	red, tall, fast, good, the
	Isaac Newton, *a famous* mathematician, discovered *the natural* law.	
verb	an action or equals word	jumps, fell, is
	I *lost* the Byron poem yesterday, but I *have* it now.	
adverb	modifies a verb	quickly, slowly, well
	The pianist played her Chopin solo *beautifully.*	
preposition	shows relationship	in, on, beside, after
	The government is *of* the people, *by* the people, and *for* the people.	
conjunction	joins words	and, or, but
	I saw the doctor, *and* she gave me some medicine.	
interjection	shows emotion	Oh, wow, yes, no, well
	Oh, yes, I always vote in the elections.	

Example

Now let's look at some sentences, and inspect the parts of speech in each one. We will use a little arrow, like this », to show what noun an adjective modifies, or to show what verb an adverb modifies.

Notice that the noun bridge is a direct object of the action verb designed.

n. adv. » v. adj. » n.

2. **Michelangelo carefully painted the ceiling.**

subject predicate

Notice that the noun ceiling is a direct object of the action verb painted.

interj. pron. conj. pron. v. n.

3. **Yes, you and I are friends.**

subject predicate

Notice that the noun *friends* is a subject complement of the linking verb *are.*

n. v. prep. adj. » n.

4. **Magellan sailed around the planet.**

subject predicate

n. conj. pron. n. prep. n. v.

5. **Alexander and his army of Macedonians won.**

subject predicate

Now, notice some very interesting things about the grammar of these sentences:

- The subject can be one word or many words.
- The predicate can be one word or many words.
- The main word of the subject is always a noun or pronoun.
- The main word of the predicate is always a verb.
- A sentence always contains a noun or pronoun and a verb.

You try it.

Here are some more sentences. Study each one carefully and imitate the five examples just presented by writing the abbreviation for the part of speech above each word, and by underlining the subject and predicate of each sentence. Identify any direct objects or subject complements you see.

1. **The scientist used a microscope.**

2. **Rembrandt slowly painted the canvas.**

3. **Yes, he and she were members.**

4. **De Soto floated down the Mississippi.**

5. **Spartacus and his force of gladiators lost.**

Check your answers against the answer key on the next page.

Answer Key

adj. » n. v. adj. » n.
1. **The scientist used a microscope.**
subject predicate

The noun *microscope* is a direct object.

n. adj. » v. adj. » n.
2. **Rembrandt slowly painted the canvas.**
subject predicate

The noun *canvas* is a direct object.

interj. pron. conj. pron. v. n.
3. **Yes, he and she were members.**
subject predicate

The noun *members* is a subject complement.

n. v. prep. adj. » n.
4. **De Soto floated down the Mississippi.**
subject predicate

n. conj. pron. n. prep. n. v.
5. **Spartacus and his force of gladiators lost.**
subject predicate

(I know, you want to know who Rembrandt, De Soto, and Spartacus were. Well, Rembrandt van Rijn was a Dutch master painter who was born in 1606 and died in 1669. Rembrandt did a self-portrait that is one of the most striking and penetrating in the history of art. Hernando De Soto was a courageous Spanish explorer, born about 1500, who is credited with discovering the Mississippi River, although the American Indians had actually discovered it long, long before any Europeans arrived in the New World. Spartacus was a proud Thracian slave in the Roman Empire who became a gladiator and who led a slave revolt against Rome. Spartacus and his men were annihilated in 71 B.C.)

Now, think about this:

One day, long, long ago, some human being uttered the first word, and language began. Over a period of time, human beings developed language, and more and more parts of speech were created, until there were eight. Use your common sense and imagination to guess what you think was probably the part of speech of the first words ever used. Think about it, and then write down your guess and the reason you think it is probable.

The part of speech of the first word ever used was ________________ .

I think this because: ____

____

____

____

____

____

____

____

____

____

____

5. Phrases: The Clever Teamwork

We all know what teams are. Five players work together on a basketball team, and each player has his or her own part in executing a well-practiced play. Cheerleaders work together to make a single pyramid, with each cheerleader standing on the shoulders of two cheerleaders below. Lawyers can work as a team to win a single case. Computer programmers work in teams to write programs; each programmer specializes in writing a different part of the computer code.

Well, by inspecting our own ideas with grammar, we have discovered a remarkable thing. Sometimes, a whole group of words will team together to imitate a single part of speech! A team of words acting as a single part of speech is called a **phrase**. We learned a bit about **prepositional phrases** when we studied the parts of speech, but now we are ready to learn more. Here is a more complete definition of the phrase: a ***phrase*** is a group of words that acts as a single part of speech, and that does not contain a subject and its predicate. For example, notice that a prepositional phrase can behave as though it were an adverb, modifying a verb:

An ordinary adverb: The penguin sat *there.*

A phrase: The penguin sat *on the iceberg.*

In each case, the verb *sat* is being modified by something, but in the first example the verb is being modified by a simple adverb, *there,* whereas in the second example, the verb is being modified by a group of words, *on the iceberg,* acting as a team to make an adverb. That is what phrases are: word groups imitating other parts of speech. It is interesting, by the way, to note that our English word *phrase* comes from a very ancient Greek word, *phrazein,* which meant "to speak."

A prepositional phrase can also act as an adjective:

- An ordinary adjective: The *top* book is a classic.
- A phrase: The book *on the top* is a classic.

There are different kinds of phrases. Let's look at some other phrases, and see some of the interesting forms that phrases can take in sentences. Remember to notice that the phrase never contains both a sentence's subject and its predicate, and that a sentence can contain more than one phrase, or no phrase at all.

Phrases

Carmen, *my favorite opera,* is by the composer Bizet.

Not remembering names is my problem.

Birds fly *over the rainbow.*

I pledge allegiance *to the flag.*

The assault team climbed the north face of *Mount Everest.*

Magellan sailed *around the world.*

Newton loved to *study mathematics.*

The painting *on the museum's north wall* was painted *by the French painter Monet.*

Conclusion

Now, let's think carefully about all of the things that we have learned. We have learned a very important secret about the way we think and express our ideas about the world. The secret is that our **ideas**, which we sometimes call **sentences**, are only complete when they are made of two parts. These two parts are the subject that the sentence is about, and the predicate that says something about the subject. If we do not have both of these parts in our ideas, we will not have a complete thought, and we will not make any sense to anyone else. Other people have to know both of these parts in order to understand our ideas; they have to know what we are talking about, and they have to know what we are saying about it.

We also learned that sometimes simple sentences can be connected together into more complicated ideas, and then we say that each little subject/predicate group inside the long sentence is a **clause**.

We have also learned an amazing secret about the thousands and thousands of words in our English language: there are only eight kinds! We call these eight kinds of words the **parts of speech**. We have learned that each kind of word has a special purpose, a function, in a sentence. Two of the parts of speech, the **noun** and the **verb**, are special, because they are in almost every sentence. The **subject** of a sentence usually has a noun (but it might have a **pronoun** instead to take the noun's place), and the predicate of the sentence always (yes, always) has a verb.

In studying the parts of speech, we learned that they are used as **parts of the sentence**. The **simple subject** is the noun or pronoun that the sentence is about. The **simple predicate** is the subject's verb. The **direct object** is a noun or pronoun that receives the action of the action verb, and the **subject complement** is the noun or pronoun linked to the subject by the linking verb.

We have learned that our minds are clever enough to collect little groups of words together into **phrases** that imitate other parts of speech, and we have seen examples of phrases acting as adverbs, as adjectives, and even as nouns (if you did not notice that, go back and look closely at the examples of phrases).

Finally, **verbs** have taught us a very important secret about ideas. Because there are two kinds of verbs, the **action** kind and the **equals or linking** kind, this means that there are two main kinds of ideas. We can either say that the *subject is doing something*, or we can say that the *subject is something*. For example, we can use an action verb and say, "The reader of this book *saw* a very good student." But if we use a linking/equals verb, we can say something even better: "The reader of this book *is* a very good student."

You Try It

adj.	n.	prep.	adj.	n.	v.	adj.	adv.	adj.	n.
The	**reader**	**of**	**this**	**book**	**is**	**a**	**very**	**good**	**student.**
simple subj.			prep. phrase		simple pred.				subject complement

complete subject ____________ complete predicate

a one-clause sentence

See if you can analyze the following sentence as I analyzed the one above:

We inspect ideas with grammar.

Check the next page for an analysis of this sentence.

Answer Key

pronoun	verb	noun	prep.	noun
We	**inspect**	**ideas**	**with**	**grammar.**
simple subject	simple predicate	direct object		

subject — complete predicate

a one-clause sentence

The Last Word

As you see, grammar is a fascinating way to think about our own thinking. By using grammar, we can examine our thoughts, and we can see how we have made those thoughts. If we did not have grammar, we would never really be able to understand how powerful our minds are. After this short introduction to grammar, however, you have begun to understand how powerfully your mind makes ideas out of language. As you learn more and more about grammar in the future, you will gain greater insight into how wonderful it is to be a human being, an idea-maker. I hope that you will always look forward to the wonderful study of grammar. It is truly a way of inspecting our own ideas.

CPSIA information can be obtained
at www.ICGtesting.com
Printed in the USA
LVOW02s1513010816
498486LV00001B/1/P

9 780757 566066